A story of love, tragedy, hope and forgiv

*"I just now finished your book, and honestly, I cannot even express the way I feel right now. I still have goose bumps. I can relate to quite a few aspects, events, and feelings conveyed in your story and truly, from the bottom of my heart, want to thank you for sharing it with me! It was absolutely something I needed to read at this point in my life, and I want you to know that you really are an inspiration, and I just pray that one day I can be half as strong as you are!"*

Jeanne Dubois, Ashland University Student

*"Your story is a compelling story of true love and your special strength. You have a gift that not only shares your hope, but also draws from those of us who only dream of making our goal to help others. I am sure Dawn and Wendy are smiling on you."*

William M. Denihan, CEO, CCCMHB

*"The life experiences and messages are a hit on college campus and among youth who are unprepared for out of left field life experiences. Katherine provides a direction and roadmap for them to follow. She's got content, personality and a passion to share the message."*

Don Philabaum, CEO, Internet Strategies

# DISCOVERING *YOUR* DAWN

# DISCOVERING YOUR DAWN

*Only when you find your dawn
can you unlock your true potential.*

*Based on a True Story by*
## KATHERINE MIRACLE

Published by Advantage, Charleston, South Carolina.
Member of Advantage Media Group.

ADVANTAGE is a registered trademark and the Advantage colophon is a trademark of Advantage Media Group, Inc.

Printed in the United States of America.

ISBN: 978-1-59932-165-3
LCCN: 2009910793

This publication is designed to provide accurate and authoritative information in regard to the subject matter covered. It is sold with the understanding that the publisher is not engaged in rendering legal, accounting, or other professional services. If legal advice or other expert assistance is required, the services of a competent professional person should be sought.

Most Advantage Media Group titles are available at special quantity discounts for bulk purchases for sales promotions, premiums, fundraising, and educational use. Special versions or book excerpts can also be created to fit specific needs.

For more information, please write: Special Markets, Advantage Media Group, P.O. Box 272, Charleston, SC 29402 or call 1.866.775.1696.

Visit us online at **advantagefamily**.com

John Kornuta

Bob Pacanovsky

Chris McManamon

Sharon R. Reed

Lynn Donofrio

Melissa Wilkinson

Tammy Brown

Loreen Robinson, Esq.

Jeff Nischwitz

Gregg Martin

Len Molloy

Shannon Reilly Gibb

**Reviewers:**

Kathleen M. Feran

Megan Priester

Hannah Houser

Jeanne Dubois

Megan Macgregor

Teresa Smith

**All income generated from this book benefits The University of Akron Foundation, Virginia Marti College of Art and Design Foundation and The Alpha Delta Pi Foundation.**

# FOREWORD

## by Kayla Miracle

As an incoming freshman in college, I have learned so much through reading this book. I never realized how relevant my mother's life could be to college students.

When I had a bad day, my mother and I would sit on my bed and talk it over and she would give me advice and share her experiences, but I never felt like she truly understood, until this book.

When you read your mother's life, it forever changes the way you listen to her experiences. Through this book and my mother's guidance, I feel ready to endure anything that will be thrown my way this year and hope to write a book of my own experiences one day. My mother did not want to publish this book, but after speaking on college campuses and seeing how it was helping students, she changed her mind.

I hope anyone reading this will share it and use it to overcome any obstacle.

# INTRODUCTION

My wish for you as you read this book is that you can see how your past can combine with your passion to create your future. My hope is that by becoming accountable for your actions, you can achieve your dreams.

When I became a college instructor, it never occurred to me that my students would share their pain and hurt. I thought the only gift I could share with students was my business and marketing experience. Though I wanted to be available and provide resources to students, I never felt that my past would or could be helpful. When a student needed me, my college agreed that I should share items that helped me when I was a student in college.

In the years that followed, I noticed three major areas where students fail. Students struggle with achieving balance, self-respect and asking for help. I struggled in these areas when I was a college student and the relationship choices I made were often dangerous. As a result, I did not deal with the guilt I carried, I was too proud to ask for help and I became dependent on other people for my happiness. In hindsight, I realize that we all have to discover our true potential or what I like to call our dawn.

Your dawn only comes by accepting your mistakes, asking for forgiveness and becoming accountable to not making the same mistakes over and over again. Over the course of the past years, I shared different concepts from this book during its development with my students. Many students said that it helped them and that they saw a bigger picture of how to respond, rather than react, to difficult situations.

This is, I suppose, why I have completed the project. At different points, I put it in the bottom drawer, but inevitably, someone would enter my life and I would find myself dragging the manuscript out, no matter how painful, in the hope that someone else's tragedy might be avoided or handled in a way that embraces survival. On the tail end of adversity or at dark fate's fingertips, I want young people to know that no matter how far they think they are in the darkness, there is light up ahead. I am proof.

The day I sent this manuscript to the publisher, a friend gave me this quote by Claude T. Bissell.

---

*Risk more than others think is safe.*
*Care more than others think is wise.*
*Dream more than others think is practical.*
*Expect more than others think is possible.*

---

His words are a template and a touchstone on how I want to live my life. If we lived our lives like this quote, we would learn from the best. We would be learning from ourselves. We would be that change we want to see in the world. There are great people of faith who have risked more than others think is safe. Harriett Tubman went back not once, but nineteen times to save more people. Mother Theresa cared more than others thought was wise. Martin Luther King had a dream that would change our world. Abraham Lincoln expected more than others thought was possible.

My challenge to you is to learn from your past and add your passion to create your future. We are stronger, wiser and more resilient than the challenges we face. Discover the dawn in your life!

# TABLE OF CONTENTS

# THE DAWN

The dawn is the anticipated light that comes after a long night of darkness. In the darkness, you can hide your feelings: those dark shadows of guilt, shame and fear. The coming dawn exposes every detail and you can either try to hide or show the world your reality. Only when you find your dawn can you be free of your shadows. What shadow do you carry that holds you back? What is it that you want, but cannot get? What could you do if your shadows did not haunt you?

It all seemed so innocent, so normal, but in five minutes, I met someone who would change my life forever. I never knew that I needed to change or be accountable. I was just moving along trying to succeed at what I considered important. I thought I was a good person. I thought that I would be strong enough to make a stand about something important. I thought I was smarter and stronger. I felt I could overcome anything. I believed I was a good friend. Evil and selfishness proved me wrong.

# WHY SHE MATTERS

As I look at her, she is so beautiful. There is something about her, a glow that lights up a room and a smile that lets you know she is true. She makes everyone feel special, and as we talk, I notice a pink streak in her hair. I love that streak and I love her name, Dawn. She is very different from most young women; she has an edge and is very bold. I admire how she stands up for what she believes in.

As we talk, it is obvious that she is genuinely interested in my thoughts. I first catch a glimpse of her compassion when she noticed the scar on my chest. I am trying to hide my scar, but today I was running late and I did not apply my normal makeup to cover this flaw.

I usually get three reactions to my scar. The first is "Oh my God! What happened?" The second is that people flash an awkward expression and then look away. The third, my least favorite, is "Did you have a bypass? My grandpa had bypass. Wow, how are you doing?"

My surgery took place when I was fourteen and I did not have bypass, so the bypass story about grandparents gets old fast. The question of what happened takes too long to explain. I would rather have people just look away.

Dawn looks at me for me, not my scar. Although I am not sure why, I feel like she knows my story. I want to spend more time with her, but in our sorority's recruitment process, our policy is to meet as many guests as possible. I say, "Dawn, I really loved meeting you and I hope you come back." That was an understatement. I wanted a "little" sister and I wanted it to be Dawn. I am equally certain I can help Dawn in her transition from high school to college.

As the weeks pass, I enjoy spending time with Dawn and eventually become her "big" sister and mentor. As her big sister, my job is to guide and protect her, but we are also having a blast. Inseparable, we go everywhere together.

Dawn shares my love of dancing and our favorite song is, "Girls Just Want To Have Fun!" We both love Cyndi Lauper and on any given night out, Dawn has everyone up and dancing! She is clever at making sure the guys she and I like are right up front so we can talk to them. This night, Dawn looks awesome. She is wearing the shirt that we share, blue and white with our Greek letters in satin. Dawn looks better in it than I do and only she could pull off wearing a jersey shirt out dancing. However, she always thinks that she looks fat and there are times I have to remind her that she is beautiful and that no one has the perfect skin and curvy figure like Dawn.

As we dance, I say, "Dawn, look who's checking you out!" Then she says, "Kathy, let's make the walk." The "walk" means that we would say hi to our friends throughout the bar both to see who was there and also to keep an eye out for those guys we want to meet. Dawn and I love meeting with friends and just dancing, but most of the time Dawn and I blow off guys so we can just talk and plan for our future.

With Dawn I can share my dreams because she is my confidant and I trust her with everything. Dawn has a special place in my heart and we laugh because I call her my gumba, which is Italian slang for lifelong friend. Dawn's family has an Italian background, so she and I picked gumba to describe each other.

I told her, "Dawn, when I was growing up I begged my mom for a baby sister. I am so grateful for you." She hugged me and I said, "As your big sister, I will always be here for you." As I said that, Dawn just smiles and tells me her goals for what she wanted to accomplish on campus so that I could later introduce her to the right campus leaders and help her find an internship.

As we meet the campus instructors and student leaders, Dawn makes an impact on people because she is smart. She has ideas to help people and her ideas are fun and creative. Dawn always gives so much of herself and always puts other people's needs before her own.

I was writing an article for the *Buchtelite*, our campus newspaper; it was a story about how campus organizations were hiring student interns. The story was boring, but Dawn is so funny in her support, "Why don't you add some drama! Kathy, take a risk! You always play your writing so safe."

Dawn is a great writer and I love reading her poetry. Watching Dawn in action, I know she will change the world through her intelligence, persistence and courage in challenging people to make something better. I say, "Dawn, let's take over the campus newspaper and change the sections to everything we like."

If someone is not having fun or is upset, Dawn is there to help them. One night Dawn heard that, in front of a crowd of people, a friend of hers from high school had been slapped by her boyfriend. Dawn visited her and the girl was talking about wanting to get back together with this abusive boyfriend. Dawn responded, "You deserve better. Never let anyone do this to you. You are a good person and you will find someone who will treat you right."

Dawn invited her to go out that night with a group of friends. Dawn helped the girl with her makeup and picked a great outfit for her so that she felt amazing. Dawn told me once that she would bring home stray animals. I could see that if someone or something were hurting, Dawn would do whatever it took to stop the pain. She never leaves anyone behind.

# THE PROMISE

As I get closer to graduation, Dawn and I make our plans for the future. We dream our dreams in strange places, including a 2:30 a.m. fast food drive-thru run and many times on the dance floor. We both agreed that we would start our own businesses. I would build my business first and invite Dawn to work on our marketing as a writer.

Dawn also plans to work in fashion and I know that she will succeed because she is always fantastic helping everyone else dress for our nights on the town. She is also so great at helping me shop. Dawn is kind enough to teach me to blend my makeup and do a better job at hiding my scar by using green makeup under my foundation. She is the only person that I ever let touch my scar.

Our promise to always be a part of each other's future and there for each other became more important as I increased my class load. I am involved in many extra-curricular activities and I have a major role in the upcoming campus theatre production. Dawn is making sure that everyone we know buys a ticket and she sends me cards everyday saying she believes in me.

Even though I now have less time to spend with Dawn, we share Halloween both dressed like Madonna. We love this evening of parties, renewed friendship and dancing! Always the dancing!

# TRUE FRIENDSHIP, TRUE LOVE

S hortly after Dawn became my little sister I met the most amazing man named Sam, who I wanted to get to know better. Sam was nice and funny and when I saw him I thought, he is so handsome. We became friends and I tried to hide my feelings, but I was crazy about him. I loved how he talked; he was loud and funny with a personality larger than life.

Sam's smile lights up a room and I love how he cares about his friends. Sam is always helping people with their problems, especially international students. Sam makes everyone feel welcome and if someone is not included, Sam will speak up to help them. My feelings for him are growing and, as much as I try to just be friends, there is some sort of chemistry between us. I am not sure why, but we seem to have a connection and he believes in me so much.

As our friendship grows I am noticing Sam sometimes lacks confidence and I cannot understand why. He has the intelligence, the personality and the looks, but there must be something deep that he will not let me see. Sometimes when we talk about him, he will tell jokes or avoid telling me about himself. I want to spend every minute with him, but I am nervous because Sam is so intelligent. He is a geology major and I wonder if we have enough in common to make a relationship work.

As I get to know Sam better, I realize that he is a loyal son and brother. Sam is the oldest of four children and his parents are first generation Italian Americans. Sam told me that as a little boy, he would help his parents with documents because he learned to speak Italian before he learned English. I love hearing Sam's stories about how he helped his siblings and parents even though he was just a child.

Sam gives so much of himself to other people and the more we talk I cannot help but want to be with him. As our friendship grows, Sam and I talk about everything but I am afraid to share my feelings. I got up my courage and asked, "Sam, I need your advice. I like this guy, but I am afraid to tell him. He is a geology major." Sam says, "Is it Dennis Giffon?" I say, "No." Sam asks, "Does this guy live in the Geology House?" I say, "No, but before I tell you, I am nervous this guy may not feel the same way I do." To which Sam replies, "Kathy, any guy would be lucky to date you." Then I knew I could share my secret, "Sam, the guy I like is Italian." Sam smiles the biggest smile and says, "Is it me?" I say, "Yes!" Sam leans over and gives me a passionate kiss and says, "I always wanted to be your boyfriend, but I never thought you would be interested in me." From that moment on we became a team with a bond that I thought could never be broken. Everything comes easy to us. We love and respect each other. Our love grows and just to have him near me makes my heart melt.

My family loves Sam and we have so much fun together. Our families are very supportive of our relationship and I love that this love story is growing like my sister and brother-in-law's love story. When I was little I watched my sister and brother-in-law fall in love and I wanted to have the same type of relationship that combined friendship and passion. My brother-in-law always protects and defends my sister and one day I saw that I had this with Sam.

I overheard Sam defend me and protect me. I belong to a campus organization that had rules of how many meetings you can miss and I overslept and missed an event. The committee planned to kick me out of the organization. Sam was talking with a guy who ran the committee and I heard Sam say, "Kathy is working a lot of hours and she just made a mistake. You cannot kick her out. If you have a problem with my girlfriend then you have a problem with me. Let me talk to the committee, and they will see that Kathy just has a lot of pressure on her right now." Sam kept trying to convince this guy but I did end up getting kicked out of the organization. When I tried not to cry, Sam held me and told me, "Listen to me, baby, you are amazing and you are better than this. You are so beautiful and your blue eyes make me crazy. I love you so very much!"

I applied for a job as a summer orientation assistant so I can live on campus to be closer to Sam. The job would be perfect for me because I love the university and I can see Sam every night!

Dawn and I have taken on new challenges over this year. Dawn is working more hours and by the time I am selected to be a summer orientation assistant, we have not seen each other as often. Dawn has grown a closer friendship with a special little sister we shared in our sorority named Stacey. Maybe that was for the best because when I found out I was selected for the summer orientation assistant job, I will not have time for Dawn. I know that Dawn often feels jealous of my time with Sam.

My personality is driven by achievement and Sam is so good for me because with him I can relax and be myself. Sam, like Dawn, understands me and brings out the best in me. Sam and I talk about our future and Sam writes to me that he cannot wait to be together forever and that he will always be there for me. We have a deep love for each other and we do so many fun things together. We love to see new bands and Sam has taught me to play foosball. We talk for hours. When Sam holds my hand I will follow him anywhere. With Sam I am safe and loved.

Sam is a musician and he is so talented, I love to watch him play and I know he has a future in music. Sam is Mr. Positive and I have always been positive, so we work well together. I am seeing Sam's confidence grow as we have built our relationship. One day I was waiting for Sam at the bottom of a staircase and as I looked up at him coming toward me, every girl on the staircase turned to look at him. It did not bother me; I just laughed because I was the only girl Sam even noticed.

Sam's new confidence made him a better student and I could see his happiness growing. I love watching him talk and I laugh when he gets loud and tells jokes. My sorority sisters love Sam. Sam and I went to my sorority formal and he won an award for helping and supporting our sisterhood. I am so proud of him and we had a blast at the formal. We danced so much that by the end of the night, Sam had to hold me up. Sam sang the words to me as we danced to the Honeydrippers' "Sea of Love." I feel so close to him like we are one person. I have never felt so close to someone. I thought about the time I got sick and had to stay in the infirmary at college. Sam stayed with me and took care of me. Even though he was busy, I knew Sam would be there for me.

Sam is a hard worker and extremely intelligent. Sam will push himself to the point of exhaustion and so many times he will take a nap and I just hold him and watch him sleep. I am so in love with him that I can just look at him for hours and dream of our future. I have always been a career girl and I had so many plans, but I want to give those up for Sam. Sometimes my feelings for Sam scare me.

I told my parents I want to marry Sam and my parents said that I must finish college and then we would talk about wedding details. As Christmas approached I wanted to give Sam an amazing gift. I knew he loved twelve-string guitars, but my budget was too small. I kept looking and asking musicians where I could find the best one. My high school friend Eddy had his dad order one from an international contact, so I could get the very best for Sam at a price I could afford. I wanted to have it engraved somehow but I did not have any extra money. When Sam opened it he was so happy and so surprised! I realized that the guitar did not need to be engraved; Sam would always know my love for him every time he looked at that guitar.

Sam comes from an amazing family. I love having dinner at their home and his family makes me feel welcome. I have so much fun with Sam's family because we talk for hours, laugh and enjoy each other. My only worry is that they are first generation Italian Americans and Catholic. I wonder if they would consider me, a very American, non-religious girl to be good enough to marry their son. Sam's family includes me in all family events and everyone is so nice. Sometimes I cannot keep up when they speak Italian, but I can keep up on the eating! I love the Italian food and they have taught me so many of their customs and traditions and I love it!

I made the decision to work on campus so Sam and I can spend every minute of every day together. I am excited that when I am done with work Sam will come see me and we can have fun over the summer. I know Sam is the one and he loves me for me. Sam never tries to change me and he is happy for me when I am with my friends. My respect and love for Sam shows me that this relationship is built on trust. Sam is never jealous or selfish; this is different from my past relationships.

My previous experience with guys had been awkward. When I was in junior high, I became ill, my eyelid was droopy and sometimes I could not speak well. Guys were not interested in me and I was considered "the sick girl." Eventually, I had major surgery to take out my thymus gland, which left me with a scar on my chest that makes me feel ugly. The surgery saved my life and I had no more symptoms of muscle weakness. By the time I entered high school I was determined to have more fun and even dated a great high school guy who was like my best friend.

My first year at The University of Akron, no one knew about my high school illness, so the door was open for me to get involved in more activities. I also felt more comfortable around guys. My high school boyfriend and I had broken up, so now as a college student I wanted a serious relationship. However, the guys I started dating took me for granted and did not want to spend quality time with me. I began to think that my expectations were too high.

Unfortunately, I am finding that again my expectations may be too high, I have not heard from Sam for weeks and I wonder if Sam is ignoring me by not calling. Maybe he does not love me the way I love him. Sam says he is always busy and I am trying to be patient. In May and June, I did not see Sam very much and now it is July. I have been feeling sick and I just need Sam.

I wonder why he is not here for me and why I am so dependent on him. I am growing lonely and wondered why I moved to Akron this summer to be with Sam. I ask Dawn, "Why are guys so confusing?"

Dawn reminds me, "Kathy, sometimes you want things to happen now and your timing is different than other people's timing. You and Sam have been together for so long, you know he loves you." I said, "I am not so sure. Sam is not calling and I think he is not interested."

Dawn always knows what to say and she told me, "Guys have different timing than girls and they don't notice the things we notice and sometimes we get hurt because they seem insensitive." I know Dawn is right. I have two brothers and Dawn is really close with her brother, so we know that guys operate differently than girls. However, I am lonely without Sam. If he does not love me I should break up with him but I know in my heart I still love him and I am sure I always will. Why does he not want to be with me? Did I say or do something wrong? Did he get bored with me? Is there someone else? Am I not being understanding of his needs?

I am friends with Sam's sister Gina. Gina is funny and she is a good person. No matter what, Gina will always tell you the truth and she will be there for you. I am so upset about Sam and so hurt that I cannot even call Gina. I know I should, but I am too hurt to talk about my thoughts of breaking up. I do not want to break up, but I feel it is the right thing for me to do.

Dawn convinced me that we should go out and she knows how to cheer me up. Whenever I feel like staying in, Dawn will pick out an outfit for me and do my makeup even though I say, "I am not going!" I have had enough of feeling that Sam is taking me for granted and I ask him to come over. Dawn says, "Kathy, think this over. Don't rush into this." As she leaves, she hugs me and I see Sam's truck pull into my driveway. I look at him and think, you are so awesome and so handsome, Why can't this work? I say, "Sam, can we talk?" and he holds my hand as we search for a place to sit. Sam says, "Kath, what's wrong?"

As I look at him sitting on the bench outside Grant Hall my heart is racing. All I can think is that I am making the biggest mistake. I say, "I think we should break up." Sam says, "Why are you doing this?" I start to cry and he holds me. I cannot answer his question. I just need to walk away. Sam hugs me and as he walks away, I feel like I am in a nightmare, the kind of nightmare where you are screaming and nothing comes out of your mouth. You cannot make a sound, but you scream because you are trying to alert someone that you are in trouble. I could not make a sound, but I wonder if I could scream, would Sam turn around? As I watched his truck pull away, I start sobbing and I realize I may have made the worst decision of my life.

My best friend Jo is working hard to cheer me up and she is so good to me. Jo is planning parties so I won't spend my time crying and staying in our room at night. This summer turned out so differently than I had planned, but I am trying to keep busy with my summer classes and meeting my high school friends in Cleveland.

It hurt to visit Little Italy in Cleveland because everything reminded me of Sam. I saw the little Italian children and I thought about what my kids would look like if I married Sam. The Italian food and traditions reminded me of Sam's family and how much fun we had. I tried not to think about my secret dream that I would go to Italy with Sam and when I heard the Italian songs, it was hard to not think about my dreams for the future. Maybe Sam did not see the dreams I saw. Maybe I was not meant to be with him. I started to feel I was not good enough and that my lack of faith and my background would not fit. Maybe I was not the type of person Sam saw as a wife. Sam always told me that my not being Catholic or Italian was not a problem, but, maybe deep down, Sam did not take me seriously.

When you are lonely, you try to hide it and act like everything is okay. I try to focus on my future. I realize how many true friends I have. I have reconnected with so many people over the summer and I know I need to move on from my past with Sam. I tried to journal but the words would not come out. I felt stupid for falling so hard and I wondered if I should go home for a few weeks to get my head together about my future. As I thought about my feelings for Sam I realized that I was willing to give up everything and I had never been a person who gave up everything for a guy. I was a career girl driven by achievement and success, but when I was with Sam I felt peace and it scared me that everything I believed about myself might be untrue. Maybe I would be happy getting married and having children with Sam. I questioned my choices and what I believed about myself.

I tried to have fun with friends and not stay home and cry about Sam. The breakup was painful, but I needed to realize that people sometimes cannot love you the way you want them to. My decision to break up was a reaction to being scared about my deep connection to Sam. Sam's family was exceptional, I never met a family who stood by each other and lifted each other up the way Sam's family did. Sam's family has a strong faith and I felt a part of their family even though I was so different. I wished I had their faith and I tried to believe, but the hurt of this breakup just made me frustrated with God.

I wanted to be part of Sam's family and be Sam's wife. Unfortunately, my decision to fall so hard for Sam cost me losing a part of myself. I knew that summer that there would always be a hole in my life and a part of my heart I could never give away.

To move on from Sam I focused on keeping busy and ignoring my feelings. I chose to bury my hurt and to not think about why the breakup happened but instead to just pretend I was happy. My goal was to be out every night with either college or high school friends, but I was surprised to see my new friend Max again. Max is handsome and I saw him at many parties. Jo was given a calendar that had Max and his friends as the covers of each month. Max was December and I kept December up all year long. I wondered if I could just have a fun relationship and not get serious then maybe I would be whole again.

Max walked into Spicer Hall to register for classes. In my job as a summer orientation assistant, my co-workers and I took turns assisting students to register for classes. When I saw Max, I begged my co-workers to let me take the next student so I could help Max! I was so nervous that when I opened my mouth to say, "Can I help you?" It just came out "Help you?" I think he thought something was seriously wrong with me. I tried to help him, but when I asked questions to get to know him, he would give me one-word answers. When he left, I thought, "Well, that was awkward."

Max came back to Spicer Hall two days later and asked for me. I was shocked he wanted to see me again; this time, I just let him talk. Max was so interesting and fun. Over the next couple of weeks, Max came back to Spicer Hall often enough that my boss said, "That guy is either really interested in one of my staff or he needs major help with his classes!"

When Max asked me out, I wanted our first date to be perfect. My friend Rhonda taught me how to make lasagna and I found a way to remove a dorm room window so we could have dinner on the roof of Grant Hall.

At the time, my friends are telling me I jumped into a relationship too soon and that I am on the rebound. Sam is calling and writing me notes about how he wants to get back together. I am so confused. I was so sure Sam was the one. How do you know who is the love of your life? Is there just one person for you? Or are there many types of love and many types of people you can be compatible with? Why am I uncomfortable being alone? If that is true, then why? I just know that no one has the answers I need and I am not going to lose Max because people feel I should wait on getting into a relationship. I also know that I gave everything I had to my relationship with Sam and when he did not call or try to be with me I learned that he did not love me the way I needed to be loved or the way I loved him.

Now that I am with Max, I am trying not to fall for him, but I am so impressed with how Max cares about people and how funny he is. Max makes our relationship a priority and we have so much fun together. Max and I both need a lot of communication and this relationship works because we agree on how we need to connect. With Max, every day is an adventure. One of the things I love about Max is watching him with Dawn. He cares about her as if she were his little sister.

About this time, Dawn really likes a guy named Tom, but it is clear that Tom does not feel the same way about her. I know that Dawn is hurt and I am trying to help her. Max always seems to know what to say. First he is telling her a funny story and then Dawn is laughing through her tears. Dawn loves Max like her older brother. Max drives us places Dawn and I love on the way home from dancing. Max meets us at our house and we convince Max that being with us will be more fun than meeting his friends at the next bar! Dawn has a way of persuading people to do things and Max knows we adore him!

Max has taught me how to do things I never imagined I would do. I learned how to repel off a building, drive stick shift and play hacky sack! Max taught me to bumper ski in winter, and he makes me laugh every day. We have been on great road trips and I take him to my favorite places. We are so bold. We trespass on private beaches. We find parks and unique places that we make our special hideaways.

I love Max's family and when I am away at college, I feel a part of something when I am at his parent's home. Max has great friends on campus and they talk about what a wonderful person he is, and I know why people love him. Max has a talent for helping people. Someone told me that Max was heavy when he was in middle school and had endured a lot of teasing. I think Max's past makes him a great listener and very compassionate.

I am falling in love with him, and I am not sure he feels the same way I do. I fear that Max is pulling away as I try to grow closer. I am taking a chance to see what Max is thinking and I am honest when I say, "Max, I am in love with you." Max says nothing and I feel so stupid.

As we drive home, we do not really talk. I am thinking this might be our last date. When Max drops me off at my house, I jump in my car and drive to escape my embarrassment. The song "Crazy for You" by Madonna comes on the radio. As I drive, this song takes me back to thoughts of my old boyfriend, Sam. Maybe I was unfair in my breakup with Sam. Did I make the wrong decision?

I cannot believe what I see. There is Sam driving in front of me! I need to tell Sam what happened and that I am sorry. I follow Sam to his friend's house and we talk. Sam reminds me that, towards the end of our relationship, he was not calling because he was busy all the time.

Sam said, "Kathy, I had to work! It was not that I did not love you, I was just busy." I felt I should give Sam another chance. Sam and I had a relationship like my parents, a real team with deep love. I have always wanted a relationship like my parents have. My family loves Sam and I can see my future with him.

I am trying to focus on rebuilding my relationship with Sam but as we spend more time together, something is just not the same and Max keeps coming back to me. I am so confused, I love both Sam and Max and I do not know what to do. How can this happen? Can you love two people?

My sister Linda is concerned and said, "Kathy you cannot have your cake and eat it too. You cannot do this. You are going to hurt both of these guys and you are going to get your heart broken." I made the difficult decision and I knew that once I made this decision I had to stick to it.

Although I ran back into Sam's arms, I eventually knew that I had made a mistake. When I told Dawn that I cheated on Max with Sam she said, "Kathy, how could you do that? Max is a great person and if you felt he did not love you, why didn't you wait to see and give it time? Not everyone is going to love you the way that you love them." She is angry with me and the look on Dawn's face tells me she has lost faith in me. Now I have lost the respect of the two people I love the most.

I wonder if I can win back Max's heart and his trust. During my time away from Dawn and Max, I need time with my pledge sister, Wendy. Wendy is always there for me and we always can have fun and relax. I need her because everyone else seemed to judge me, but she always understands. Wendy and I went to the Akron Agora nightclub. I tell her my story and she gives me great advice.

As we danced and talked, I notice so many guys looking at her. Wendy is gorgeous and many guys ask her to dance, but she is sweet and never makes a guy feel foolish for asking when she says no. Wendy is polite and thoughtful and when I was president of our pledge class, she always had my back. I am lucky to have such a loyal friend. Wendy is modeling the next day after our night out and she is so funny as we eat a half-pound of M&Ms and stay up until three o'clock in the morning. Only Wendy can look so amazing at seven the next morning for a photo shoot. I, on the other hand, have to walk in shame and ask Max to take me back.

When I met with Max, I nervously admitted to him my mistake. When I had said that I loved him and he did not say anything in reply, I thought he did not want to be with me. Max says, "I just was not ready to say I love you yet. I do know that I love you and I do want you back." I feel so lucky he has taken me back, but I fear that with Dawn I might not be so lucky.

Dawn and I finally spend some time talking and she expressed compassion and support for me. We talk about our goals for the upcoming school year and we agreed that I will run for head of recruitment for the university and she will be a recruitment counselor. Our plan is that we can spend time together working on recruitment and I can focus my weekends on Max to rebuild my relationship with him. It seems like our plan will work.

Max and I are growing closer and as our love grows, we make a pact to always be there for each other and to believe in each other. Max is considering walking on for the school's football team. I know he can make the team and I am using one of my connections to learn more about how we can make this happen. Max is an excellent athlete and I love going to watch Max play intramural football, volleyball and even wrestling.

Max eventually decided not to walk on for football, but he knows that I believe in him. I wanted to cheer Max up after he made the decision, so I invite him to a date party. Only Max and I could get into trouble before a party even begins. "I dare you to jump in. I know you won't do it!" I said, as we stood in front of the bubble-filled E.J. Thomas Fountain. "The bubbles are so high that if you jump in you will get lost and I will never find you, but I dare you!" As I said this, Max picked me up so that we fell into the fountain and we were covered with bubbles. We kept kissing to not lose each other, "I cannot believe you just did that Max!"

Max laughed and said, "You know that I cannot walk away from a dare." We were soaked, but we did not want to miss the party so we ran home, put on dry jeans and raced over to Clay's Park. We danced all night and did our usual sneaking off when no one was looking. We climbed to the top of a waterslide to camp out under the stars, that is, until the park police caught us.

Max is the life of the party and because he is fun, guys and girls love him. I feel people miss something about Max that I know is important. One day it was clear that I was right, when Max told one of his friends how to fix an engine and his friend did not listen. I enjoy Max's friends, but sometimes I think that they only see Max as a party guy while missing how smart he is with a gift for finding solutions to problems. I have heard people say that a person's greatest strength can also be their greatest weakness. Max is blessed with good looks and personality, but sometimes people do not respect him or see his wisdom. He can find a solution for everything from mechanical problems to people problems. Also, Max never judges people; he just listens and helps them to find a solution.

As a couple, we have our arguments and sometimes I should show Max more respect. I see how it hurts Max when people do not respect him. I try to listen and not to judge his actions. We always come back to each other and when we need to, we hold each other accountable or as Max calls it, "a boot in the behind." We give each other a push to get back up when we are down or when we need to work on something. I see other college couples struggle and say awful things to each other, but one late night I saw what I never wanted to see.

Max and I had pulled into a parking lot to talk about the next day. Max was saying, "When I get to Hudson, I will call you..." when we heard a cracking slap and we looked up to see a young woman hitting her boyfriend. She started screaming at him and would not stop slapping him. Max and I knew this couple and it made me sick to my stomach as she continued hitting him while he cried and pleaded with her to stop. For some reason I knew he would not hit her back. I wondered what was so wrong that she was so angry and why he did not walk away.

I felt guilty just watching and doing nothing, but we knew that this couple fought often and it would embarrass the guy if he knew we saw them like this. I know Max wanted to do something; he was always the hero. Often he would step in when people needed help, but this time we had to pretend we did not see it.

When the couple finally made up, I thought, "How can they stay together?" Max and I agreed to never hurt each other. Our pact was to always be there for each other and when I was sad or upset, I would lay my head in a place between his shoulder and neck and he would put his arm around me. It was safe there and I never wanted to leave.

As winter approached, my class load would increase with the start of my second major. Max and I had planned to celebrate. Max took me to our favorite restaurant, Whiteys, to eat Maggie burgers and drink beer. I never expected a romantic question to be asked over beers, but I was so excited when Max gave me his fraternity lavaliere and we committed to always being a team.

As we drove home, the snow was slowly falling below a full winter moon. Getting out of his car, I saw a big patch of untouched white snow that the moon made glisten like diamonds. I looked back at Max and smiled, waved and fell back to make a snow angel. Max jumped on me and we laughed and threw snow in each other's face. As I looked up at Max, the moon was above him and I ran my fingers through his dark wavy hair. We held each other to keep warm and as I looked into his big brown eyes, I knew that nothing could ever come between us.

# PRESSURE

As the fall semester classes started, I realized I was overextended, but I felt I could keep it together. The academic advisors and my professors tried to talk me out of my plan to complete so much in so little time, but I was too proud. When I needed help, I would not ask for it. I just slept less and gave even less time to Max and Dawn. Everyone needed to realize that I was older and that I would soon graduate. I felt my friendships and love for Max were strong enough to endure anything and, so far, I was right. My best friend Jo had graduated and had a great job. I missed Jo so much, but seeing her as a professional woman made me think about what I needed to do to be ready.

A snowstorm was my break from this pressure. As classes were cancelled, Max made our day one of the best I had in college. Max taught Dawn and me how to bumper ski! We hung onto the rear bumper of his Cutlass as he drove through the parking lot for hours with us sliding, screaming and laughing behind. It was just like the old times with the three of us laughing and doing crazy stuff, but then the police told us to stop!

This release of the pressure of classes was good for us and I wanted our time together to never end. I had no idea how the pressure would continue to build or how I could become someone I never wanted to be.

I was nominated for an internship at the local TV 5 and was in the running for an investigative reporter position with a small, community newspaper. I was planning student recruitment for the University of Akron and was the vice-president of a major campus leadership group. The fires were burning and while I was able to put them out, I never dreamed that even bigger fires were coming. I tried to hold all of my obligations together, but Max grew disappointed, Dawn grew distant and I could not understand why everyone wanted so much from me.

My father had always told me to take off the rose-colored glasses and see reality, but I could not see the bigger picture of my life. I chased after all those accomplishments and forgot about my supportive relationships. When all the balls I was juggling started to drop, I felt that I was not good enough. I had come from a strong family with brothers and sisters that were achievers and leaders. My father expected a lot from me and my mother always wanted me to do my best. I was not making anyone proud while I was trying to be so perfect.

Max tried to help me, but my confidence was beginning to waver. I had so many goals and while I wanted my goals to fit into Max's goals, he did not seem to know what he wanted. I grew frustrated with him. The things that I loved about Max, like helping me to relax with no set plans and just living in the moment, now aggravated me because I needed to have a plan to be sure I would graduate on time and be prepared for the future. Maybe I was missing the signs, or maybe I did not want to see them. Our relationship had changed and I did not understand why. I just needed him to wait for me until I was done with college and then we could have more time together.

# CALM BEFORE
# THE STORM

My favorite time at my favorite place all led to the sad moment that happens once a year. It was the end of summer, which meant my last trip to say goodbye to my solitude and the only place I could seem to reflect and escape.

In the sunset, the water sparkled like diamonds while the beach grew quiet. I knew it was time to leave and my thoughts turned to what this year would bring. This was to be my last year of college, the completion of two degrees, my leadership of student recruitment and my internship.

As I packed up to leave the beach at Mentor Headlands, I looked back one last time as I did every August, thankful for my special place to think and relax. I always felt ready for the upcoming school year when I made my final visit, but this time I was plagued with a sinking feeling.

Driving to Cleveland, I thought that perhaps I was just nervous about dropping off my resume at TV 5. Why was I nervous? I had changed into professional clothing at the beach on the chance that I might run into someone who wanted to talk to potential interns. Maybe I felt uneasy because I was finally graduating or because I had decided to complete two degrees. Earlier I had convinced my academic adviser that I could handle a double load of credit hours for the fall and spring semester. As I thought about my upcoming classes, I tried to comfort myself that I was an A student with only a couple B grades and that I was committed to extra study.

My last view of beautiful Lake Erie was the turn on Interstate 90 just after the MLK Highway. This would be my last glimpse until I graduated in May of the next year. Pulling up to TV 5, the security guard took my resume and wished me luck. I really wanted this internship, as I knew that my goal to produce and write could happen if I just got in the door at a local TV station.

My parents had been supportive of my borrowing their car to get back to Akron, but I had to return it in two weeks. This helped me to take my mind off the dread I was feeling as I thought about the upcoming Labor Day holiday and the chance to see my parents one more time.

Maybe my dark feelings stemmed from the chance to see Max and to try to work out our last argument. The drive to Akron was long, but I planned to use the time to figure out why Max and I disagreed all the time.

As a senior in college, I knew it was time to finalize my career plans and to cut down on social events. On the other hand, Max constantly pushed me to cut back on leadership activities and to relax. My own expectations often stressed me out and I always felt that I needed to achieve more. Max had my best interest in mind, but I often pushed my expectations on him.

As I pulled in my driveway on campus, I realized that part of my uneasy feelings had to be that I was late to meet Max. I had stayed too long at the beach. I saw Max standing with roses in his hand, but looking at his watch. I felt so bad because he was welcoming me back to Akron and had driven back to campus even earlier to see me come back. Our classes would start in two weeks after Labor Day, so while we had some time to have fun I also had meetings with my team to finalize campus recruitment.

Those weeks were a whirlwind of meetings and phone calls to ensure that every detail was in place. I ran to the printer to pick up University of Akron's first ever recruitment guide. It was the first publication I had ever led from concept to completion. I had a clear vision for this publication. It had been an opportunity to work with an amazing team to sell ads, takes photos, write and produce.

As I held the initial copy in my hands, it hit me that I had to thank Dan, the editor of the yearbook. When I had started this project, I had no idea what I was doing. Since Dan was writing a story about student recruitment, he helped and listened to my vision. Dan never tried to change my ideas, instead, he challenged me to make the project better.

In my race to meet deadlines, I met with Dawn to discuss the student recruitment committee that we were in together. I was jealous because she and Wendy had become very close and, because I did not have time for Dawn, I felt that she had gotten closer with Wendy to replace me. I also knew that Dawn felt unimportant from all my time spent with Max.

In our meeting at the student center, Dawn told me she had missed a committee meeting. I exploded, stating how she had been selected as one of twelve women to serve on a recruitment committee.

I reminded her that over 120 women had applied and how important it was to attend every meeting.

I only backed off when I really looked at her and realized how bad she looked, exhausted and sad. I knew she was angry with me as I said, "I know you're mad, but it is my job to keep the committees running." I walked away and never looked back thinking, "I have too much to do to make sure my own little sister makes every meeting."

I needed to focus my thoughts on what an exciting time it was to be back on campus. I loved the University of Akron and I was blessed with many friends who had the same goals I had. The student leaders were all working to get ready for the year. We all wanted this year to be successful and to promote the university we loved.

I wanted to make my last year the best one, so I accepted a nomination to the Senior Board. I went to a meeting and, to my surprise, Dan from the yearbook was also selected. I was so grateful to see him. I showed him my final copy of the recruitment publication to thank him, knowing that he cared about my work and what mattered to me.

When I walked back to my house, it seemed like the campus had grown smaller. I could name a friend in every building and I enjoyed seeing faculty and administration. I wondered how it would feel to leave Akron and all my friends at the end of the year. This year would begin with something special happening and I could feel it.

As Labor Day approached, I realized that my plans to meet Dawn and Wendy for a night at the Harbor Inn would not happen. Dawn had not called me since our fight at the student center and I was not about to call her. I deserved an apology.

My parents called and we arranged for me to drop off their car, have lunch and say goodbye. I needed Max to follow me to my parents' home to drive me back to school. Max said it was too far and that he did not have the gas money. I was so disappointed and I lied to my parents saying that I needed the car for another month for my internship.

The Sunday night before Labor Day, Jo and I went to the Harbor Inn to celebrate the end of summer and the beginning of my senior year. I confided to Jo about my fight with Dawn and how I was mad at Max for not agreeing to go to my parents' home. I thought Max wanted to break up with me, and Jo was the only person who I could talk to about my mistakes in the relationship.

At the Harbor Inn I had hoped I would also see Dawn. However, this guy kept approaching me to ask about Wendy. He was concerned, saying that Wendy was supposed to meet him and that he was now worried about her and Dawn. I wasn't because I figured that Dawn was avoiding the Harbor Inn so as not to see me.

For Labor Day the next morning, I drove to the beach alone, feeling a sense of escape from the pressures of my relationship with Max. I could see how all the qualities I loved about Max I had also tried to change. I wondered how he would break up with me.

The beach was packed with the holiday crowd and I felt lonely all by myself while everyone was talking to friends, playing volleyball or swimming. I even ran into a friend of Max's, which made things feel worse as I acted as if Max and I were still the perfect couple. It seemed clear to me that Max did not feel the way I did and did not love me.

My thoughts were running through how I would confront Max when I looked up to see him in front of me smiling, "I wanted to surprise you!" Max was so nice that day and we both apologized for everything. The wonderful feelings of making up and his words made me feel that we could start over. We left the beach hand-in-hand, but as I looked back at the water, that same sense of dread hit me again.

On the drive back to Akron, I reflected on why I still felt uncomfortable. I could not understand what was bothering me because I felt that my life with Max was secure. When I drove onto campus, I saw a car that reminded me of Dawn's and I thought that I should call her. I needed to apologize and ask her for forgiveness.

# THE EVENTS THE DEVIL LOVED

As I pulled near my sorority house onto Spicer Street, there were police cars everywhere with lights blinding my eyes. I knew something was wrong and my heart raced. When I walked into the kitchen, my sorority sister Jill seemed nervous and she asked me if I had a good day and asked me what I had done. I felt she was trying to stop me from asking questions. As I told her how Max surprised me, I tried to act normal while I felt like the room was spinning with the heavy feeling that she was hiding something.

When I saw Stacey, my other little sister, it was clear she was supposed to be the person who told me what was happening. Stacey followed me up the stairs and asked me to sit down. Stacey told me that the police had come to our house and that they wanted her to identify two young women: one blonde and one brunette. I held onto my chair, but felt myself sinking.

Stacey explained that once the police had looked at the group picture of our sorority sisters that they had pointed out Dawn then Wendy. My heart was in my stomach as Stacey said, "Dawn and Wendy have been murdered and the killers have covered their tracks." My heart began pounding and I could not hear anymore. As my stomach cramped up and I felt I would vomit, I ran to the bathroom and sat helplessly on the floor. I tried to throw up, but sat shaking with my thoughts turning, "Stacey was wrong, it was probably some other girls that they found."

Stacey followed me and I asked her, "Are you sure?" She repeated, "The police wanted me to go to the morgue because Dawn had a key chain with our letters on it, which is why the police came to our house."

I stumbled to the phone and called Max. When Max answered I could not tell him what had happened. I just started crying and said, "I need you. Please come to me." He was at our house in what seemed like three seconds and I heard Jill tell him what happened downstairs. Thankfully, Max ran up to hold me and just listened as I repeated what he already knew.

I called my parents who were worried that I lived in the same sorority house with the killer still on the loose. I was paralyzed by fear and could not drive the distance to my parents' house with classes the next day. I then called Jo and she comforted me, but I wanted her here with me. Max held me so I could stop shaking, whispering, "Baby, I am so sorry, I cannot believe this is happening. I am here and I will always be here for you."

As the night grew into morning, I could not sleep and Max walked me to the bathroom because I could not be alone. I was not strong enough to walk down the hall and I was scared to be by myself. I told Max that maybe the police were wrong, maybe Dawn and Wendy were just on a road trip and that it was like the time that Dawn ran out of gas and we had to go help her. Maybe she was somewhere and she would come back tomorrow. Max pulled me into his shoulder, the place I always felt safe, but this time I knew that even Max could not protect me.

I had not eaten nor slept when Max helped me get ready for our first day of the school year. As I walked on campus, many students did not know about the tragedy yet and some of them looked so happy for the new school year. I remember looking at their new outfits and how they were hugging each other in reunion. I could not believe how they looked. How could they be happy? How could they smile?

As the news spread by that afternoon, we learned more about what happened. Dawn and Wendy were driving under a city bridge when some men threw a rock that broke the windshield of Wendy's car. Dawn and Wendy did not know that those men were the same strangers that later came to "help" by offering their unsuspecting victims a ride. That night, my friends were kidnapped, tortured, raped and bludgeoned to death.

When I found out everything that had happened, I hated myself for not being there for Dawn and Wendy, as a friend should. I thought that if I had been with them, I could have stopped them from accepting the ride.

Our campus was filled with people talking about the murders and I witnessed people who did not even know Dawn or Wendy act as if they had been good friends. I overheard some guy say that he had been dating Wendy at the time, which was a lie. I still had not slept or eaten and the pressure of sitting in classes while acting as if nothing had happened made me angry. I had to escape, but as I walked through campus, I felt like I was drowning.

The walk from my last class towards the sorority house was a long journey full of tears and anger. I called Max because I was afraid to walk alone with the media swarming our house. I questioned why I wanted to work at Channel 5 and a newspaper. Why did they have to ask so many questions?

As I mourned alone in my room, I went through a basket of college pictures and mementos. I found a small plaque that I received from my high school boyfriend's family at my high school graduation. I cried at its reminder of my high hopes for college and the future. I could no longer believe this quote as I read:

### Blessings for Going Away to College

*May the autumn leaves carpet beneath your feet*

*And the angels lead you through the class day maze.*

*May your homecoming time be extra sweet*

*And your heart warm with Indian summer days.*

*Like Jesus may you grow in wisdom, age and grace.*

*May you learn to read and write and think and sing,*

*May you swiftly run in knowledge's rapid race and*

*God's kind love to all your roommates bring.*

*May God hold you in the palm of His hand until*

*We meet again and keep you safe and well.*

*Father, Son and Holy Spirit*

This plaque had proved to be a lie, and it made me think of the last time I had seen Dawn's mom. She had said how excited Dawn was for the upcoming school year. Now, our hopes and dreams were shattered. I was here and my friends were dead. Why was I left behind?

I thought that if I had been with Dawn and Wendy, I would have been able to stop them from taking that ride. My friends were dead and I could have prevented their murder. I had caused the fight that prevented me from being with them that night. My job was to protect and guide Dawn and I had failed.

Our Alpha Delta Pi sorority had an emergency meeting at the house with alumni coming to help and counsel us through this. I did not want to talk and I told people I did not need their help. We watched the news together and I was mad because the report focused on what Wendy was wearing: a white leather mini skirt and jacket. I asked, "Why does what she was wearing matter?" Watching the news and seeing Dawn and Wendy's pictures made it even more real and proved to me that my secret hope that the police had found two other girls instead of Dawn and Wendy would never be true.

In the days prior to the funerals the media reported details of what happened, and I worked very hard not to listen. I would not let anyone tell me what happened, but I was walking to a class and overheard a guy say, "Dawn was stabbed in the neck." My heart dropped. I began to cry, but I did not stop and kept walking. This guy had recounted the gruesome facts like they were nothing! He did not even sound upset, but just so matter-of-fact.

People who knew of my relationship with Dawn tried to tell me things about the murders. I was angry because people were weirdly intent on giving me things Dawn had owned or telling me what they knew about her. This only coupled my anger with frustration. When I wanted to talk about the good memories of Dawn and Wendy, no one else seemed to want to.

The calling hours and funeral were painful and I felt guilty, knowing that I was supposed to be with Dawn and Wendy that night. I did not know what to say to Dawn's mother. I could not imagine her pain. I hated myself for not having the courage to tell Dawn's mom that I was supposed to be with her daughter the night of the murder. I was a coward. Others who knew I should have been with Dawn and Wendy seemed supportive, but I was sure that behind my back they were whispering quietly about why I did not go with the girls that night.

I looked around the funeral home to see the same people, from parties the weekend before, crying and holding each other. I had a flashback from a year earlier when Max and I had trespassed on a private beach. The beach was called Utopia, Max and I jumped the fence to watch the sunset. That night a group of people came asking everyone if they had seen a group of girls. An older man, who was obviously upset, looked at Max and me like we were criminals as he asked us if we had seen these girls. He kept saying that, "They are among the missing."

I still do not know why, but Max and I laughed about this later. From then on, whenever we were at a party and a friend was late, we would describe them as "among the missing." As I realized that Max and I had become that older man from the beach, it was not funny anymore. We were struggling to understand what had happened to our friends, why we were here and why our friends were dead.

As I stood looking around the funeral home, it seemed that although these friends and I may have been young, in the past five days, we had become old, angry and sad. We could trust nothing in this world. We were all close, but suddenly we were facing reality without rose-colored glasses and our lives would never be the same.

We were forced to handle something we had never dreamed of. We did not get to say goodbye to Dawn and Wendy or show them the love they deserved. None of us had imagined that we would be cut off from them so soon. Dawn had always smiled and lit up a room, but now the world was dark.

My world had been turned upside down and I wondered why everyone I deeply loved was ripped from my life. My dream of Sam was destroyed and my dearest friend Dawn had been brutally raped and murdered. How could this happen? Did God hate me that much? Was I being punished? Dawn was my friend who was honest with me and made me a better person. Dawn always told me I helped her but at the one point in her life where she needed me the most I was not there.

At twenty-two years old to lose your friend, who was twenty years old, made no sense and my grief took over. How could everyone at this funeral just sit there and not scream? How could the men who murdered my friends be allowed to live even one more day? Toward the end of the funeral I began to break down. I could not control myself. Max wiped tears from my eyes and held me up so that I could make it through the day.

After the funeral, a group of my other friends talked about how God could let something like this happen. One of the girls said to me, "Sometimes God wants to get your attention." I did not know God, but if this was the way he wanted to get my attention, then I had no trust that God even existed. I hated him for letting this happen to my friends.

My pledge sisters took me to Wendy's calling hours and it became too much for us to handle: two sisters and too many tears. We were supposed to be mature and supportive of the families left behind, but it was all too hard and we were too young to know what to say.

When we could, my friends and I escaped to the car to talk. I said, "We will never be happy again." I thought about why people wear black and felt that I would dress in black from then on.

As I tried to return to classes, I was depressed and could not get out of bed. My sorority sisters knocked on my door to encourage me to get up. My roommate tried to help me, but I became mean as my hate grew. I started picking fights with Max and I treated him like my personal servant. My rage and problems were weighing on him. I remember finally looking at Max and seeing how sad and exhausted he looked.

The year before Max had mentioned that he wanted to quit college and travel. I thought he should have gone so that he would not have to deal with all of this mess in my life. My moods were dominated with anger, sadness and frustration. It was clear to me that everyone lies and does not want to admit that life was full of pain, hurt, guilt, regret and anger.

I just wanted to be at my parent's home and forget all that had happened, back to the day before the murders. I needed to suppress this and forget it. When I tried to talk about it with friends, they would listen for awhile before getting bored. After all, we were college students and everyone wanted to have fun. People did not want to deal with such deep conversations. I also hated myself for fighting with Dawn and placing my boyfriend and myself in front of my relationship with her. I had failed as a big sister who was supposed to protect and guide.

I finally went to my parent's home the first weekend after the funerals and it helped to be with my family. I trusted no one except my brothers and sisters, Max, Jo and my Mom and Dad. On the last day with family, I could tell my parents were apprehensive about my return to college. They gave me their best car to keep for the rest of the school year and as we said goodbye, my mother's eyes filled with tears. I could only imagine what she was thinking.

When I returned to Akron, I needed to make calls to my committee to ensure we were ready for recruitment. One of the committee members also happened to be an old girlfriend of Max's. When I called her to confirm the details for the week, she asked if I knew what had happened with her and Max over the weekend. Sensing that this was something important, I pretended to have talked with Max and told her I wanted her side of the story. She told me that she and Max went on a date and kissed. I tried not to cry and quickly said goodbye before calling Max.

I thought that Max would apologize and beg me to stay with him. I could not have been more mistaken. Max told me that he needed more time to think and that we should break up. I was devastated, but fought to hide my shattered heart from my friends and family. I did not go to classes, but just stayed in my room or the library. I wondered why God had left me here and why I was not with Dawn and Wendy in that car that night. I was paralyzed with fear. I now hated God. My parents had taught me to be strong, but I was not.

My sorority had planned an on-campus memorial service for Dawn and Wendy. The plan was Max would drive Dawn's family to the service. I wondered if Max would still show up. Our sorority president Amanda was an amazing leader. Not only did she plan the service, she also told me not to worry if Max did not show. She consoled me because she knew how much I lost in my friends and Max.

Max did show up to help and he was great with the families and very kind to me. It was hard to see him, but I knew he would know what to say to comfort Dawn's family. The memorial service was difficult and media were everywhere. I was broken and scared. I could not hide my pain so I just broke down. It was all too much and to return to classes the next day was overwhelming.

I was pursuing a double major with twenty-five credit hours. I was in charge of recruiting over 1,000 women for the entire University of Akron sorority system while being involved in several other campus activities. Everyone was depending on me, yet I was overwhelmed, sad and afraid. My sorority sisters came to me to try and help, but I assured everyone that I was okay.

I was required to speak before 200 campus organizations in representation of the Greek system. Here I was a student leader who needed to be the perfect role model. However, there were times I would leave the room after giving one of these presentations and hear someone whisper, "Isn't she in the sorority where the two girls got murdered?" Every night, after every speech, I would cry the entire way home. It hurt for people to talk about my friends as only the girls who were dumb enough to accept a ride from strangers.

I hated Max for breaking up with me, and I made sure everyone knew how awful he was for cheating on me. I conveniently forgot I did the same thing to him the previous year. I had become a victim and believed the worst of myself because it was easier than dealing with everything else. I was helpless, hopeless and knew that I would never recover. I saw Sam and his new girlfriend every day when I went to class, and Sam was very nice and was supportive because he knew how much Dawn meant to me. When he hugged me to console me, my heart dropped and it was crystal clear to me that I made the biggest mistake breaking up with him. Sam would have never broken up or cheated on me three days after my friend's funeral. Between seeing Sam and his girlfriend, Max, people talking about Dawn and Wendy it was just too much and I wanted to escape.

I had become numb to my classes and no longer wanted to learn. One professor who I knew from the previous year said to me, "I looked up your grades and see that you have gone from a very high GPA and successful college career to failing my class. Why don't you care about your future?" I responded, "I don't care what grade I get in your class, I just need to pass so I can graduate." He just looked at me as if I was hopeless. He was not wrong.

I continued to be nice to people to their face, but I gave no one my trust. I had placed a wall around myself and I would use people for my benefit. I had decided that to move on and make it through this year that I needed to hide my feelings and act as if that fateful Labor Day had never happened.

I learned how to hide my feelings from a conversation with a girl I met my first year in college. Her name was Cassandra and when we became friends, I had noticed sadness about her. Finally, Cassandra opened up to me saying, "My cousin was murdered and our family had many bad things happen at once. I felt cursed." As Cassandra went into the details, I agreed with her that her family was cursed. How could so much happen in such a small period of time? Now years later, I understood what she meant about hiding all the details and the pain.

I felt a part of a unique group, those people who had lost their loved ones through murder. People who know about your tragedy, but have not lived through this type of tragedy, seldom know what to say. They seem to feel you could just move on if you would only talk about it. On the other hand, if you act too happy too soon or if you only want to discuss the good memories about your deceased friends, they think that you are insensitive. Cassandra taught me how to hide my pain and to act as if the tragedy had never happened.

In time, I tried to be more sociable and even to start dating again. I was genuinely searching for happiness, but I could not give anyone my trust, which left those relationships with men very empty. I never thought I would be happy again.

Can you imagine living your life knowing you would never be happy again?

# A CHANCE
# AT HAPPINESS

I still wanted to follow through on my commitments to speak on campus and to work on Senior Board projects. It helped me to be with people who were going to graduate and I was excited to see Dan again on the Senior Board.

I was looking forward to the meetings just to have a chance to see him. I was happy talking with him. Dan was a great listener and I respected him. Not only was he very smart, he even helped me with my other classes so that I again wanted to learn. I started to feel that Dan and I were growing closer and his friend even confided in me, "Dan is crazy about you." This thrilled me, because I was crazy about Dan. When Dan asked me out and I became his girlfriend, I felt as if he had picked me up from my horrible life and this was my chance to be happy again.

Soon after, Max would come to visit me and tell me that he missed me. I was so confused. Why now? I had been selected for a TV 5 internship at the same time I was hired by a local newspaper for an investigative reporter position. I was so proud to be Dan's girl-friend, and I became very dependent on him. I finally felt like my past was behind me and everything I worked for was coming together. Sometimes I could not help but feel guilty for being so happy. On one level, I think I feared this success because everything was happening so fast.

The case for Dawn and Wendy was wrapping up and it was again a major issue on campus. Would Richard Cooey, one of the assailants, receive the death penalty? I felt guilty for not going to the trial and I tried to not hear details because it hurt too much. I kept myself away from the courtroom. Sam went to the hearings and he told me some of what happened.

As I needed something constructive to do, I worked on a campaign to put a fence along the edges of the bridge where Wendy and Dawn had been kidnapped. This tragedy had all started when those men had thrown a rock off that bridge to hit Wendy's car and I was again forced to wonder how something as simple as a rock could be the beginning of the loss of my beautiful friends.

I had seen Cooey's picture when he had been captured, and I was sure that I had seen evil. I felt so bad for Dawn and Wendy's families, but I needed to be away from the talk about the verdict. Finally, Dan came to me and carefully, so as not to hurt me, told me the court's verdict that Cooey would get the death penalty while Clinton Dickens, the other murderous assailant, would get a life sentence to prison. I did not feel any better knowing that none of this would bring Dawn and Wendy back.

Shortly after the case closed and before Dan had to go out of town for a convention, he came over to bring me breakfast. I did not have any makeup on and the scar on my chest was showing. I was so embarrassed and I did not want Dan to see it. The scar continued to make me feel ugly and inadequate. Dan had not seen the worst in me, as I had hidden my anger and hate about what had happened to Dawn and Wendy. I had tried to show Dan the better sides of me, but my true feelings were still inside.

In my time alone while Dan traveled, I started thinking that I was not good enough for him. Dan had a strong faith and I hated God for what happened to my friends. I had not grown up going to church, so I felt I was someone who was not good enough for God. I had made many mistakes and I did not respect myself. What did Dan see in me? Dan had important responsibilities on campus and a very difficult major. My needs often seem to weigh heavily on Dan and I hated myself for not being able to be strong enough on my own.

The second night Dan was gone I went out with friends to a club where our friend Tim was the DJ. Tim played a song he had played when Dawn and Wendy first died. The song was "Don't Forget Me When I'm Gone" by Glass Tiger and he dedicated it to Dawn and Wendy. The music took me back to how I felt at that time, so I drank to feel more relaxed and drank again to let the pain of the past melt away.

Max eventually showed up at the club and was very attentive to me. Now, I looked at Max thinking how much I wanted him to love me. I told him about my embarrassment that Dan saw my scar when he brought me breakfast and Max replied that he accepted me as I was. Max and I had a bond from going through some of the worst moments in life. Max knew the real me and had always accepted me as I was. In my anger about Dawn and Wendy, I had treated him so horribly. Maybe I had chased him away and caused him to cheat. After all, I had cheated on him with Sam a year earlier and Max had forgiven me.

I was not sure if I drank too much or that I did not feel very well to begin with, but that night Max had to help me out of the bar.

Just as we were leaving while Max held me up, I looked over my right shoulder and saw one of Dan's friends angrily looking back at me. The next day I woke up not remembering my evening. My friends told me that everyone seemed to know what had happened the night before including my drinking and leaving with Max.

Bad news traveled fast and I felt that I should have worn a scarlet letter while walking through campus that morning. The night before had made me look bad and people would believe what they wanted to believe. Everyone loved Dan and I was the girl who had "cheated" on him.

Later as I approached Dan, I could tell by the look on his face that I would not get a second chance. I wanted to explain, but all that came out was "I am not good enough for you." It was the truth that I did not deserve someone as awesome as Dan. I will never forget the look on his face; I had disappointed the one person who pulled me up when I was at the lowest point of my life.

After we said goodbye, I walked away, but looked back hoping that Dan would turn around. Dan never looked back.

# LOSING MYSELF

Returning to classes, I found that I again could not focus on my life through the mess of hurting so many people. When I began to date Max again, I blamed him for all my problems. I felt that Max had stayed at college that spring just to take care of me, and I knew I had spoiled his dreams of travel. I was not a good girlfriend and although Max tried to make our relationship work, I became distant and we argued more and more. I became mean and my hate grew. I began to smoke cigarettes to relax and quickly became addicted. I had no idea that it would later take many years to quit this habit.

Max was unhappy and I knew it. My words and expectations hurt him. I did not respect myself enough to give him space and try to make it on my own. I think my dependence on him was killing him. I knew I needed to make it on my own.

I decided that Max was too good for me. I had an addiction to nicotine, was failing two classes and felt trapped in a personal prison. I couldn't trust anyone while I was stifled under my survivor's guilt for Dawn and Wendy's death.

How did my life come to this? How, in one year, could I transform from a girl who was an A student, friendly, fun and from a good family into a hateful person who accepted the worst from myself? My parents did not raise me to be this person. My parents expected a lot from me and I was failing.

I kept missing classes. I needed help, but was too proud to get it. The faculty and staff at the University of Akron could see the change in me and I was blessed when they stepped in. One of my professors took the time to call me and say, "I need your talent in this class." Her call helped me to get out of bed and come back to school. I needed to find a new way to study so I could focus. I created a way to learn that helped me memorize parts for plays. Now I was able to not just memorize facts, but to actually know and implement what I had studied. I started working harder to handle all my classes and to balance my life. Besides my professors and the academic advising staff, my mentors, Dr. Dudley Turner and Tom Vukovich, helped me pull myself together and finally graduate.

It was a miracle that I made it through that last year of college! Max never gave up on me and he had a sixth sense about my needs and when I was in trouble. After the long struggle to graduate, Max bought me a beautiful bracelet that said, "I love you." Not only was it beautiful, but also because Max and I had been through so much together, this graduation gift was so special. At the graduation ceremony, I looked up at Max in the audience and I was holding my wrist to show him the bracelet. I wanted him to know how much I loved him and that I was committed to our relationship. I was trying to get my life together, but nevertheless the shadows still haunted me.

# FIGHTING FOR MYSELF AND MY SOUL

As I started my first job out of school, I continually tried to get my life back on track. I found a cute apartment with a fireplace, and I tried to make it a home for Max and me. I had confided about our relationship with a woman at work who told me that, "Most couples never endure a tragedy like you and Max have lived through. The tragedy will either bond you or break you."

I was committed to making our relationship work, but I knew Max was unhappy. I wanted more from our relationship than Max was ready for. I still had trouble focusing and I kept getting speeding tickets. This collection of tickets led to ten points on my license and a court appearance in which I needed my parent's insurance card. I blamed everyone else for my problems. Finally, my selfishness and lack of support for Max's needs led us to an argument that cost me everything.

I had told Max that I was mad at my father for not giving me money for my apartment and the insurance card I needed for my court appearance. I had never realized that a comment about my anger at my father would have such an impact on Max.

Max told me that I was selfish because my father loved me and did so much for me. Max continued angrily saying, "Kathy, you are selfish and no matter how much someone loves you, they will never meet your expectations." Then the words I never wanted to hear came as Max said, "I want you out of my life." My heart dropped and I tried to speak, but Max pushed me and it was clear that I was out of his life.

Who had I become? Why did I push Max to change? Why was I so dependent on him? I needed to let Max live his life and I needed help for my own. I ran to my car. That night was the last time I ever saw Max.

The breakup was devastating and I hated being alone in my apartment. I had trouble moving on. My heart longed to be with Max and I could not stop crying. I kept hearing the song, "Against All Odds", by Phil Collins and the words "take a look at me now, there's just an empty space, you're the only one who really knew me at all" hurt because I had thought we were the couple who could survive anything.

I started praying every day that Max would come back, asking God why Max was not with me. In the past when we broke up, Max always came back. Now Max only called to check on me and it was hard to talk or act strong. Max is a good person and he never leaves anyone he cares about, so I think he thought we could be friends.

When I dated again, my choices were not healthy. I used people. They say when you look for the bad, you find it. I found it by dating a man who I felt really loved me. The attention I received made me feel better now that Max did not love me the way I wanted him to, so I ignored all signs that my new romance was dangerous.

At first, I passed off all of his jealousy as deep affection and his emotional abuse as my screwing up, yet again. However, when he took me to meet his parents and they were not home, I knew I was in trouble. He yelled at me for asking where his family was and when he grabbed and hit me, I thought about the couple fighting that Max and I witnessed. I remember how I had thought that the guy should leave and not take that abuse. I decided I needed to run. He caught me and told me to hold still and I could only think of Dawn and Wendy. I pushed him off me and I ran out of the house. I never saw him again.

I decided to never let that happen to me again and I made a pact with myself about what I will and will not allow in my future. I decided to create a personal code of ethics. I was now alone and had to depend on myself to turn my life around. I wondered how I could confuse love with attention and why I needed the approval of men.

This time I had to make it on my own and get to know what I wanted and valued. I also knew that I needed to find what I believed in. I needed to value and learn about myself. I needed to stop running from myself and to make myself whole. My love for Dawn made me whole and I always felt God sent her to fill that place inside me that needed and wanted a little sister. On my own I needed to fill that hole that was left when Dawn died. I needed to stop reacting. I needed to start thinking things through before responding.

I was lonely and it was hard to not have someone to lean on, but I was not going to jump into another relationship and depend on someone else. I guarded my heart and became my own advocate.

My college roommate and sorority sisters were worried about me, so they took me to a Good Friday service at St. Bernard's Catholic Church. As the service began, I reflected on everything I had lost that past year, my friends, my boyfriend, my confidence and my happiness. I would give anything to go back to the day before that Labor Day.

I kept thinking:

*"What if I hadn't argued with Dawn?"*
*"What if I was with Dawn and Wendy that night?"*
*"I should have been there, but if I had, could I
have stopped their murders?"*

---

I cried because the way I had handled my grief led to hurting Max. My anger and my blame ruined my life. I had tried not to cry as the service started, I watched the story of how Christ gave his life for me, but I wept realizing how selfish I had been to hate God after he sent his son to die for me. My new peace with God strengthened me.

Now I was on a mission to be happy and rebuild my life. I started accepting invitations with guys to go out "just as friends." I volunteered, joined a gym and took fun classes. I became my own advocate and I wanted to change my name from Kathy to Katherine. I loved the name Katherine. My dad always called me Katherine the Great when I did something good. I needed to remind myself of that name again, because I was not happy with how I had handled my past. My new name would reflect my new way of dealing with life.

I also adopted Don Henley's song, "Heart of the Matter," as my song to move on, because he sang about carrying anger and how it could eat you up inside. I realized the song was right, because it is about forgiveness even if someone does not love you anymore.

I began a journey journal and I created questions that would have helped me at the time of the murders. I realized I had been so unprepared and dependent upon unrealistic, rose-colored glasses to get me through life. After the murders, all my innocence was gone and those rose-colored glasses flew off. I knew that I needed to fight for my happiness and reach out to people instead of pushing them away.

I noticed that I began saying encouraging things to people. When I would say goodbye to people close to me, I would say, "You know I love you, right?" Or if I was not sure someone understood what he or she meant to me, I would say, "You know how much you mean to me, right?" At first, I did not know why I said this and then one of my co-workers noticed saying, "Did something happen to you when you were younger?" I said, "No, why?" My co-worker replied, "You say things like you've lost someone and when we are in parking decks you look around like someone is trying to get you. You always watch your back and it makes me wonder if you endured a tragedy."

Well, my truth had to come out. I decided if it was that obvious, that I should tell people I work with so they can understand why I continually watched my surroundings or why I have trouble driving under the bridge where Dawn and Wendy were kidnapped.

I still had issues with fear that came out one particular night at a party. I was talking with a group of people when a drunk guy picked me up and playfully spun me around. When he would not stop spinning me, I thought he was going to hit my head on some kitchen cabinets. I went into a panicked fight or flight mode. Because he would not listen when I yelled for him to put me down, I clawed his back with my fingernails. I may have overreacted, but I think I will always have some kind of fighting response if I am scared.

Painful memories never leave you. One night in my workout class, my instructor pulled me aside after class and asked, "When you do the jabs and hooks, you have the most intense look on your face.

What are you thinking about?" I told her, "I think about the men who killed my friends and how I would defend myself if I were attacked."

I felt that my fears may still have been too strong, but I was blessed when I had a boss who said, "People have a right to their feelings." That statement helped me to realize that each person handles feelings in their own way. I also think that people who put a timeline on their feelings are the same people who say stupid, condescending comments like, "You will forget about this in time."

Two years had passed since Dawn and Wendy were murdered and I was spending more time with my best friend Jo and having fun again. Jo helped me escape my lonely apartment and introduced me to new people. They say your friends are the ones who will be there when love leaves you. I realized that Jo was the one person who would never leave me or fail me.

My friend Gina and I later reconnected and I found out something that shocked me. Gina had worked with Dawn and Wendy that fateful summer and Wendy had invited Gina to go with them the night of the murders. Gina said she did not want to go and she had a bad feeling. Gina's decision saved her life, but she too carried guilt. Gina told me that her brothers and family talked with her and helped her to move on. Sam and Gina's family was amazing and I could see from dating Sam years before that Gina did the right thing by opening up and accepting help. I realized I should have talked with my family when they asked me how I was doing. I should have opened up to someone and sought out help.

As the fall approached, I thought that I needed to take down the walls I had put up and try to move forward. I had no intention of dating or having a serious relationship. I planned to focus on my career and plan for my future business. However, a simple invitation from someone from my past changed those plans.

Craig Miracle invited me to an Elton John concert and I agreed to go just as friends. Craig intrigued me because I had seen him six years before and I remembered my first impression. When I was a freshman in college, I had a class in East Hall, a beautiful old church on campus. One day I glanced down from the second floor to the playground in the back of the building and I saw this handsome blonde man playing with the kids. I remembered thinking, "What a special guy!" The kids loved him and they would pull and jump on him while he was so fun and sweet with them.

I had no idea that this guy was Craig Miracle, an education major who was working at the daycare center and trying to raise his own son as a single dad. I later saw Craig at some college parties and I developed a bit of a crush on him, although I had heard he was divorced and spending every other weekend with his son. As a college student, I did not want to pursue a relationship with someone who was divorced with a child.

When Craig invited me to see Elton John, I thought that we would have a blast because we had become friends. I was hoping Craig would not consider it a date because over the past those two years he had asked me out many times as we had conducted business together. Craig decided to buy his father's awards business and I loved watching him work with people. Craig would listen and help people create awards and gifts that were unique and beautiful. I saw Craig help many people who wanted to create a memorial for their deceased friends. I loved his compassion and understanding. Craig is truly loved by his customers and I know he understands their feelings.

However, I had continually declined his offers because I had wanted to get my life together without, once again, depending on a man. Now that we had been very open with each other about our dreams and our past, I felt more comfortable accepting his invitation.

The Elton John concert was incredible and when I ran into people I knew, I was very proud to introduce Craig. I had to wonder why I had never accepted dates with him before. Here was a great man who I was crazy about and I was pushing him away. I now hoped that he would ask me out at the end of the concert and I was so excited when Craig asked me, "Do you think we can become best of friends and best of lovers?"

Craig and I had so much in common with major tragedies in our lives and overcoming feelings of inadequacy and self-doubt. As our love grew, we spent as much time together as we could. We would stay up until four o'clock in the morning talking and laughing. Craig was so fun and I wanted to be with him every second of every day.

I admire Craig because he is resilient. When he was younger, he had been a great football player until he endured an injury that would force him to never play football again. Instead of staying angry, Craig moved onto basketball and although he was not the tallest member of his team, he was an amazing player who helped take his team to state.

I knew Craig and I could overcome any obstacle together. Craig and I had survived a long, tough road to find each other. Craig even chose a song for me called, "Back On My Feet Again" by The Babys, because he said that I picked him up out of his dark time after his divorce. However, it was Craig who brought me happiness, love and joy.

Some of my friends were concerned that I would become a step mom at a relatively young age. I wanted to be helpful to Craig and to help my stepson become a great man, but I was concerned because I did not know anyone who was a stepmother. I asked God for guidance. My stepson, Joshua, is so fun and very smart. I knew that Joshua was destined for greatness and I wanted to do everything I could to help and support him. My love for Craig and Joshua grew every day. Craig, Joshua and I would go on hikes and picnics. Our time together made me realize I wanted to spend all my time with them. We grew into our own little family.

Craig and I had been dating for three months when I was offered a great job in another state. The job offer meant a major move, but this was a strong company that could launch my career. However, in my heart I knew I could not go and the decision felt easy with no struggle or question of what I wanted to do. I kept my decision to myself to see if Craig felt the same way that I did. One sunny afternoon I visited him at work to tell him about the offer, "Craig, P&G offered me a job. I would have to move to Pennsylvania."

He got tears in his eyes and I knew Craig felt the way that I felt. I then told Craig I was not taking the offer and he held me. We both started crying and it started to rain. We just held each other until we were soaking wet, but I never wanted to let go. I knew that this was the moment when we both realized that we would be together forever. The sun was so bright through the rain and I knew at that moment I would marry Craig, I could see my forever in his eyes. I knew that no matter what difficult times I would face, Craig would be my partner, lover and friend. My commitment was to never put Craig second. I knew that during my past with Max I had often made him feel that he was second to my goals and activities. As Craig and I grew closer, I began to pray for him daily. On the day we married, I promised God that I would cherish Craig forever.

As for Craig's relationship with God, his faith was beginning to grow as he was mentored by a very wise man named George Hilty. At first, I thought that George was weird when he kept calling and trying to talk to me about Christ. Then George prayed for us and took Craig to men's seminars. Craig also went to a weekend retreat with George and returned different and at peace. He was becoming an even better husband, but I was still worried at this change. Craig was very slow in his approach to me about faith. He never pushed his beliefs on me although if I asked him any questions, he would answer them in a way that I could understand.

Due to my past illness, Craig and I knew that my chances of getting pregnant and having a healthy baby were small. However, when I actually became pregnant, we prayed that we would be strong enough to endure whatever happened to both our baby and me. I went to church by myself when Craig was out of town and I asked God to help me and to give my baby every chance to be healthy. I did not ask for safety for myself as I felt that God had already given me a second chance. I told God that I knew I had been spared for some reason. Perhaps it was so I could have this baby.

Two weeks later God blessed us with a healthy baby girl. I wanted to use Dawn for her middle name. However, Craig and I agreed that we should choose the name Evelyn because Craig's grandma Evelyn was ill and it would mean so much to her to have a namesake.

As Kayla Evelyn Miracle grew, I knew my daughter never needed the name Dawn. She had the most important part of Dawn. She had Dawn's passion and determination. Kayla is bold yet compassionate and, trust me, she is not afraid to fight for what she believes in. Watching my daughter interact with people and take care of her friends makes me smile and laugh because God has blessed me with Dawn's personality in Kayla.

When Kayla and Joshua were old enough to understand, I told them about the deaths of Dawn and Wendy. I begged my children to be careful and to understand that if they were late or if I did not know where they were, then I would not have a normal reaction. My children and family know that, due to my past, I always fear the worst.

Sometimes people ask me if my faith grew out of a tragedy. I share with them what I remembered from the service I attended that Good Friday after Dawn and Wendy's death. I realized then that God has a plan for me. The plan may not always go the way I want it, and sometimes my prayers are not answered the way I would like them to be, but I know God is walking beside me every step of the way. I am still angry that Dawn and Wendy cannot share the moments of my life, like my wedding and the birth of my daughter, but I now realize that I must live each day as a gift. When bad things happen I may not understand why, but I know that I trust God.

I believe my sorority sisters, Sam, Max and Dan were sent to save my life. Craig was sent to save my soul and God helped me save myself. I have learned that life is not about accomplishments; it is about relationships. I have been a part of teams and experiences that have helped me grow. I have tried to encourage and help others. My faith has helped me see those moments of joy, compassion and miracles that I never knew existed. I have been blessed to have an incredible husband, give life to my daughter, grow a nonprofit, build a business and teach college students to appreciate themselves while teaching them new skills. I am blessed to have the opportunity to encourage and help a stepson, mentor future leaders, love my step grandchildren and save my own life by releasing me from my addiction.

I thank God for my life, each and everyday. I realize that I have been given a second chance. I know I have to make the most of each day and opportunity because Dawn and Wendy did not have the chances I have had. My prayer is that Dawn and Wendy would be happy with what I have done with my life.

# REFLECTION

It has been twenty-two years since that fateful summer and I am now a business owner, public speaker and college instructor. I am honored to have the opportunity to teach interns in my business and to educate and encourage college students.

When I see a student with a bruise or if they seem to be upset, I make myself available to them. I am amazed how many college students will tell instructors what is happening if you just ask, "How are you doing?" As an instructor, I help students find the resources they need to get help. I have students write me a note on the first day of class, asking them to tell me what they expect of me and what I need to know about them. Some notes tell me details that are about injuries that may not be noticeable, but some notes are about a personal crisis that they are in and they often tell me they are homesick. Instructors are on the frontline when it comes to identifying and helping students in crisis. I was blessed that my instructor took the time to call me to motivate me to come back to class.

I am blessed to work with the Virginia Marti College of Art and Design faculty and staff who work hard to get students the help they need or to keep an eye on them in crisis. In our society, college students report feeling increased stress from taking on too much or getting into unhealthy relationships. Many college students run away from their responsibilities or consider suicide. The pressures on this age group are intense and my hope is that this book and the following resources will help these young people.

Richard Cooey's defense team shared the teasing and bullying Cooey endured and how that led to his anger and frustration. The dangers of teasing and bullying dominate our elementary, middle and high school classrooms and continue to be a problem in our society. My challenge to all readers and myself is to consider how we can help. I have recently volunteered and am a speaker at the Cleveland Public Schools. My hope is to make an impact and encourage students.

I have not shared my view on the death penalty, but will share the facts surrounding Richard Cooey and some personal items that have affected me since the fall of 1986. Over the years since Dawn and Wendy were murdered, local and national media has covered the case and resulting sentence. I have kept all the clippings and have now read the exact details of the murders. My heart breaks at every newspaper article and new piece of evidence that is released. Every year, my husband and children know that I am not okay over Labor Day.

People always tell me that they remember the story and that they are so sorry. As each year passes, I hate that Dawn and Wendy are defined by their deaths and not by their lives.

Dawn and Wendy were amazing young women with very bright futures. The plans they had for their lives and the impact they had on so many people while they lived are often forgotten. I have met people who did not know Dawn and Wendy, but after seeing their story realized how precious life is. Many parents share with me how they tell their kids how to be safe, followed by telling their child about Dawn and Wendy.

The people who really knew Dawn and Wendy understand the impact they had on our hearts and, even as time passes, it does not get easier. We were forever changed. An act of evil altered us forever, and the beautiful gift of Dawn and Wendy was taken from us.

The attacks on two innocent women are not excused by Cooey's claims of an abusive childhood or the use of drugs the night of the murder. The fact that Cooey admitted to smoking pot in prison for seventeen years shows me that our system must change.

I was sickened when Cooey made the news with another victory that his life should be spared. As my husband and I worked hard to build businesses, Cooey studied law and used his persuasion to convince legislators and Judge Dan Polster (who granted a stay to Cooey in July of 2003) that lethal injection is cruel and unusual punishment. Cooey is evil and his connections helped him to escape from prison on a February morning in 2006. Cooey hid under a snowdrift and almost got away.

Cooey seems to have a power of persuasion that allowed him to manipulate reporters with false information. He had become so popular that blogs about him and media coverage makes his words travel the world.

I have tried to block out his presence, but on a day that my company held a press conference for a client, we received the front page of the metro section, which was dominated by an article on Cooey. It often seemed that I could not escape Cooey and I felt that he used his evil to keep himself alive long after other death row inmates had been executed. I was challenged by the words of Dr. Martin Luther King, Jr., "He who passively accepts evil is as much involved in it as he who helps to perpetrate it. He who accepts evil without protesting against it is really cooperating with it." I could never just look away from evil.

In 2008, I contacted Dawn's mom to apologize for not being there for her during the time of the murders. Dawn's mom has been an inspiration for me. I enjoy emailing with her and the chance to reconnect with her has been an answer to my prayer. So many miracles happened in 2008, although when the events happened, I did not see them as such until later.

A series of events happened to get me ready for October 14th, 2008, the scheduled execution date of Richard Cooey. In fall of 2007, I was asked to give my testimony, which was very difficult, but helped me to put into perspective what had happened, and how I had to deal with my past. My goal was to help Dawn and Wendy's family in any way they needed. I was not sure what that meant, but I wanted to help.

In early 2008, I kept having nightmares about Cooey. He was in the news again and even mentioned on "The Tonight Show" for being too fat to execute. It seemed that the number of stories about him had led the public to forget about his victims, Dawn and Wendy.

As a speaker, I present specific ideas on how to develop a professional, positive attitude and I stress the need to learn from your past. As I added to this book, it helped me to stop blaming Max for my mistakes and look at the truth. In my past, I did not value myself and I needed to realize that just because someone does not love you the way you want him or her to, this does not mean that you are not worthy of love and happiness in your future.

In January of 2008, I began my master's degree program at the University of Phoenix. The program challenged me and forced me to ask myself some difficult questions about my business, my future and especially about myself. I never expected my past to haunt me in an MBA class.

My favorite faculty member, Ivy Bates, taught my favorite class, Project Management. Ivy represents what Phoenix is all about, teaching students the reality of our coursework and how to apply what we learn in the real world. In our last class, Ivy shared that you can be the best project manager, but if you are not willing to improve yourself then you cannot be successful.

Then Ivy asked the class a profound question, "What is your shadow? What is it that you carry that holds you back? If you removed that shadow, what could you achieve?" I realized that night that my shadow was the guilt I carried from my past. I realized the journal I had been writing about the worst time in my life was my way of healing and reconciling the shadows of my past. But my secrets were still hidden and I had never asked for forgiveness of the people I had hurt.

In April of 2008, my husband had a dream that I needed courage and we wondered what that meant. I had been growing more anxious as the media was covering Cooey's request for clemency. I was not sleeping well and I became even more resentful of the media coverage that highlighted Cooey. My prayer was that someday Dawn and Wendy would be remembered more as the beautiful women they were than as tragic murder victims.

I had a dream in May 2008 that Dawn and Wendy were alive and lying in a hospital wrapped in white blankets. The dream was beautiful and I was at peace because the families, my sorority sisters and I were holding Dawn and Wendy. In the dream, we were so happy and I felt the warmth of everyone holding my friends and me.

In the months leading to the execution, I ran into many people from my past and I wondered why all of this was happening. While attending events and growing my business, I happened to see Dan, who was very kind, although I still felt bad about the past. I wanted to ask his forgiveness, but instead we talked about business. I wanted the courage to talk with him about the past, but I just could not find the words.

In the moments after one of my speeches, I was asked why I was not with Dawn and Wendy the night they were murdered. This was a question that had haunted me for twenty-two years! The person who asked that question later apologized for asking me. However, I came to realize not only how much this person helped me to come to terms with it, but also to prepare me for the hard-hitting questions that would come from the media.

As the date of Cooey's death drew nearer, I met with my pastor, Jim Winkler, to learn of ways that I might emotionally and spiritually process the execution. I needed courage and my pastor helped me to define why I needed to go to Lucasville. With his guidance, I came to understand that it was important for me to be there for the families. I knew that the death of Cooey was all over the media and that there would be people who would judge me for going, but I felt at peace with my goal to do whatever the families of my friends needed.

As the clemency was denied and it appeared the execution would happen, Dawn's brother gave my contact information to the media for a story about Dawn. I never imagined the family would need me to do this, but I felt honored to share memories and pictures of Dawn. Some questions were very difficult and, once again, I was asked why I was not with Dawn and Wendy the night of the murders.

My sorority sisters, Tina and Mandy, did a great job sharing memories and our love for Dawn and Wendy to the media and everyone we knew. Mandy and Tina helped me so much because I was struggling and the memories were flooding back. As one story was published, several followed and, finally, my prayer that the girls be remembered as more than murder victims was answered.

Some questions from the media were very difficult and again I was asked why I was not with Dawn and Wendy the night of the murders. That audience member who asked me that question after my earlier speech had no idea how much she helped me prepare for the media.

As we continued to plan our trip to Lucasville, I was not sleeping well. Initially, I had tried to avoid an interview with Fox News, but eventually, I was glad that I listened to Stefani Schaefer of Fox. The story turned out to be an amazing tribute to my friends and another answer to my prayers. So many people I did not know approached me to say how they understood who Dawn and Wendy were because of the interview.

The story featured the Greek paddle Dawn had made for me as my little sister and many people asked about the quote on the paddle. The quote Dawn chose for me from Susan Polis Shutz was:

---

*There are many people who we meet in our lives. But only a few will make a lasting impression on our minds and hearts. It is these people we will think of often and who will remain important to us as true friends.*

---

The Fox story made my friends real to people during the media frenzy about Cooey. The following is what I wrote to people who supported and approached me about the story:

*We are now home!*

*Lucasville was quite an experience and I want you to know how much you mean to me.*

*My goal was to be there for Dawn and Wendy's families and help in any way I could. In 1986 when Dawn and Wendy were murdered I was in shock and I was no help to anyone. Since I was supposed to be with Dawn and Wendy that night, I had survivor's guilt and I just tried to cover up my feelings. This week I needed to be strong and do what the family needed me to do. The family gave my name and number to media and in the last forty-eight hours, I have worked with four TV stations and ten newspapers. The questions were often difficult and each interview takes me back to the day my friends were murdered. Craig had a dream in April that I needed courage; none of us knew what that meant until now. All of you helped me to be strong and to tell the story of Dawn and Wendy. Cooey's story has been everywhere and I need you to know that I believe God is the only judge. My trip was to support the families, not to engage with protestors.*

*Our journey to Lucasville was filled with concern for how the protestors would treat us and as we drove that night, it was to a spooky full moon over a very strange town. We then realized the place we were staying had protestors. We stayed at a Super 8 Motel, and this was a big step for Kayla and me, because we are not Super 8 Motel fans!*

*We roughed it out and I could not sleep, so Dawn's mom and I kept e-mailing!*

*At Lucasville we had to share a parking lot with protestors. There were four of us and about fifty of them. The Plain Dealer reported today that a busload of people would arrive to be on our side, but that never happened. Protestors approached us and said very unkind words and one protestor had a sign that upset me.*

*Lucasville was eerie and a strange, pure white dog with a huge cut in its ribs ran right past us. It was creepy how the dog barked at us but never approached. Kayla felt it represented Justice; the cut on the side represented the imperfection of the system. For me the dog represented the angel of death.*

*I was getting upset thinking about what Dawn's family was going through in the execution room. This day would bring death and details of the murders. In some ways, it felt like it did in 1986 at the time of the murders. I was reliving everything in my mind. Then our angels came, Connie, whose husband was a prison guard involved in the Lucasville riots, and two male retired prison guards. Connie had a peace about her and I felt like God sent her to me because I was getting tired of explaining the details of Dawn and Wendy's murder to reporters.*

*Connie and the guards explained what was happening and it helped to have them with us. When we saw the funeral limo take away Cooey, I did cry, but as the limo turned away, I thought, "How could you do that to my friends?"*

*Dawn's family asked the prison guards if we could come to them and they let us hug the family. I cannot tell you how good it felt to hold Dawn's mom. She has suffered so much.*

*No matter how you feel about Cooey or the death penalty, please know Dawn and Wendy were amazing women and you helped me be strong to tell their story. I realize that it could have been me, the night my friends were murdered and I am thankful for my life every day.*

*Please know how much you mean to me and that you are a blessing to my life. I am thankful to God for my life and I am blessed with an amazing husband and a very special daughter, who would go to Lucasville to help her mom through a very difficult day.*

One of my staff said to me after the execution, "Katherine, one sin can cover the world." Sin hurts so many people. It is clear to me that I am one of many who hold Dawn and Wendy in our hearts, but like the scar on my chest, I hide what is inside. It is easier to cover your feelings and cover your pain, but again like a scar, it shows. I tried to hide my shadow of guilt, anger and pain for so long that I thought no one saw my pain.

When I started teaching, it was thrown in my face. If I was committed to helping a student who needed to learn from my past, I had to make the choice to share or hide the truth.

My choice to be there for the family of Dawn led to some criticism from people who oppose the death penalty, but I had to make a stand to speak out about my friends. In the past, I had been a coward and did not stand up. Instead, I blocked out the hurt, pain and loss.

My goal now is to right the wrongs I made in my life. I will do this because my friends never left anyone behind.

During the week of the execution, Max came to mind. I was still angry with how I had handled my relationship with him. On the night of the execution, I was shocked to see an e-mail from Max. My first reaction was to tell him that he broke my heart. I discussed with Jo, Tina and Mandy what I needed to do and decided that I needed to apologize for my actions. I also needed to thank Max for taking care of me back in 1986.

God continues to work in mysterious way. It helped me to e-mail Max as he was the only person who really knew me then. Max's words encouraged me during a very difficult time. My husband and I agreed that I needed to ask for forgiveness and I am so thankful Max contacted me.

When I asked Max to forgive me, he was amazing and supportive. When I told him I was surprised at how easily he could forgive me, Max said, "I just don't hold a grudge." I realize now that I was not as strong as Max because I did hold onto grudges. I needed to continue reaching out to some of the members of my family with whom I was angry.

In the months after writing to Max, I was able to rebuild many of my relationships. My goal had become to give radical forgiveness and to strive for relationships that are strong and will last through good and bad times.

I thought the toughest person to ask for forgiveness would be Dan. That turned out to be one of the most amazing God moments. I had met with Dan again on business and, after a lot of prayer, I asked him for forgiveness. I wondered if he would think I was crazy to wait twenty-two years to do so when we had already done business together. However, Dan was so supportive and showed me so much grace, "Katherine, I just don't hold a grudge." I was shocked that Max and Dan had the same words.

When I told Dan about this book and how my teaching had led me to help college students with the issues of balance, self-respect and asking for help, he was excited and wanted me to move forward with it. Dan felt that this book is a gift from God and will help many people. Honestly, I was still struggling with possibly not publishing this book and Dan's words reinforced what I knew I had to do.

In the final weeks of my MBA program, I had an amazing professor named Dr. Vernisha Browne-Boone. Dr. Boone expects the best from her students and because I wanted the same from those I taught I felt I needed to tell her that my work in her class had not been my best. I felt that I was slacking because I already had a 3.94 GPA and this last class coincided with the final deadline for this book. Dr. Boone is an excellent professor and I did not want her to feel that I did not care.

As I spoke with her, the conversation reminded me of the professor I had studied with in my undergraduate program who approached me after Dawn and Wendy were murdered. That professor had reached out to me and although he did try, I shut him out.

Dr. Boone not only showed me she believed in me, but she also showed me a way to work smarter, so I could give my best both to this book and to her class. I strive to be a professor like Dr. Boone, who cares and gives students the resources to succeed both in life and in their studies for future careers.

I am thankful to the students who heard me speak and asked, "Is there a book?" These last four years I have e-mailed pieces of this story as well as the resources. That feedback became the narrative for this book and I hope the resources I have compiled at the end of this book are helpful.

Nevertheless, with all that in mind, my pride continued to get in the way. I did not want the dawn's light to hit me by publishing. I was still not prepared for the truth to be out. Ultimately, I had to discover my dawn in order to stop my shadows from haunting me.

As I speak, teach and consult, I meet so many people who share their shadow or their struggles and I know that they need to learn from their past. The process is not easy and you may be surprised at what you learn. I knew that I needed to face my biggest regret. I needed to ask Sam to forgive me and tell him the truth about what happened to me.

Sam is a great man and he has great faith. When you tell someone you wrote a book and oh, by the way, "you are in it," you never know the response. Sam was amazing and he will always have my respect and admiration. My actions hurt him and although he would never say it, I should have been patient with him. I should have been available to him. When you love someone, you should never leave them.

The struggle to open myself up and to showcase my past has often been stressful and embarrassing. The time I have spent looking at my actions also makes me angry and sad. The risk of exposing your past is great and if the decision to publish was about what is best for my reputation and my pride. I would never let this book see the light of day. The final choice to help others was sent to me from above, although I realized that by publishing this book, I would have to pay a price. That price may be in the form of embarrassment and questions of why now? There might also be questions about my actions or lack of action. I have often wondered what my purpose is and why I am here while my friends are gone. Maybe this work is my purpose? A wise department head named Geof Pelaia asked this question, "What price will you pay to know your life's purpose?"

I am ready to pay my price. Are you?

# RESILIENT

Are you resilient? Do you honestly look at the failures in your life and learn from them? When I work with corporations, the CEO or vice president will often tell me that their people need motivation and I am hired to motivate, inspire and provide resources. What I often find is that people do not use their past or their failures as a source of motivation. I teach them to question how we, as a society, motivate ourselves. We look at our biography or résumé and boast about all the things we have accomplished. I teach people to be proud of their success but use it to help their company and help other people.

I ask my clients to think not only of how they have helped people and their company, but also to look at their failures. I help them understand what lessons they have learned from their mistakes and how they are better because of them. I help people learn from those times that they did not get what they wanted. There are lessons to be learned from failure. When we complement our passions with what we learn from our failures, we create a future that allows us to discover our dawn.

We often think that we are a great help to people when they tell us that they did not win a contest or get the job they wanted by offering a conciliatory response of, "Oh, it's fixed." Most of the time, if we look deep enough, there is some reason that the job was not a good fit for the person or a reason they were not selected, but it was not the time to win or be chosen. Resilient people learn, improve and move on.

There is no doubt that my failures have taught me more than my successes. When I became accountable and took responsibility, I began to achieve more and I worked smarter, not harder. The people who are resilient become their own advocate by valuing themselves, balancing their lives and not being too proud to ask for help or take the time to help others.

When I reconnected with Dawn's mom, I eventually admitted to her that it was my fault that Dawn was in the car that night and that, ultimately, I was the reason Dawn was dead. When I revealed this, Dawn's mom, in her wisdom, grace, love and compassion, told me what I needed to hear for twenty-two years. She told me I should not carry such a burden and that she was sorry I was carrying that burden. Dawn's mom is so resilient, she has so much faith and she is so good. I thought I was helping her by reconnecting. I wanted her to know I would do anything for her and her family. I quickly realized that she did not need me as much as I need her.

It took me years to see that I needed to open up and learn from my past. I spent too much time beating myself up with guilt and shame. I did not value myself, my body or the memory of my friends by focusing on what I did wrong. Dawn and Wendy would not want me to avoid help or to not value myself.

When I stopped smoking, I thought back to why I started. I started smoking shortly after Dawn and Wendy were murdered. Did I smoke out of anger, fear and rebellion? I made a decision I was not good enough for the man I loved and I never asked him what he thought. I hurt friends because I was angry. I did not ask them for help, I just shut them out. I chased after accomplishments and let my relationships fail. I chose to date someone dangerous in reaction to not being with the man I wanted to be with. Why would I make a dangerous choice like that?

In the end, I needed to learn that to truly honor Dawn and Wendy's memory meant not to focus on the evil that had happened to them so much as to focus on who they were, why they mattered and to learn about them from writing this book. Dawn and Wendy never left any one behind and I won't either.

In the moments after completing this book I turned on the radio to relax. The song playing was "Don't Forget Me When I'm Gone." Dawn and Wendy, I will never ever forget you. I promise.

# TOPICS TO CONSIDER

I believe that negative emotions led me to allow abuse to enter into my life. I hope that you, the reader, will recognize the dangers of how I reacted instead of responding to the situations in my life.

- Guilt

- Not recognizing the danger of jealousy

- Accepting others' views of what is beautiful

- Pride

- Self doubt

- Dependence on others

- Addiction

- Emotional abuse

- Stress and overload

- Fear of success

- Buying into negativity

# MY PERSONAL CODE OF ETHICS

I commit myself to the following personal code of ethics:

- I will not allow anyone to treat me with harm.

- I will recognize that jealousy can be harmful and dangerous.

- I will set up a schedule that gives me time to complete my classes and homework, work schedule, family and friend time, as well as physical and civic involvement activities.

- I will secure the help I need and use my mentors to help me achieve my goals.

- I will not have a relationship with anyone who pushes me to do anything I am uncomfortable with or requires me to change for his or her benefit.

- I will give grace and forgiveness to those who mistreat me, but not allow anyone who continues to mistreat me or my family to be a part of our lives.

- I will inspect what I expect by looking at my actions to be sure I am doing what I need to do to ensure that I meet my expectations.

- I will expect a lot from myself and not doubt my ability to succeed.

- I will accept my flaws and work on the ones that can be improved.

- I will not buy into negativity.

- I will not fear success.

- I will respect my career and myself.

- I will not depend on others for my success and happiness.

- I will not put my body at risk by becoming addicted to any drug.

- I will ask for forgiveness and release guilt.

# HOW TO SURVIVE A BREAKUP

As an employer, college instructor and friend it has been sad to see people go through a breakup. You can see the signs and struggles even when someone says nothing. I am a college instructor and professional speaker, but I am not a counselor or doctor. I share these 12 steps with you just because they worked for me. I hope it helps you!

**Step One**

After a breakup, try to journal and keep a log of your feelings and thoughts. If possible, try to get closure. For me, I spent too much time wondering why the relationship did not work instead of moving on. Sometimes you cannot get closure right away. If you cannot get closure, understand that your future is what you need to focus on.

**Step Two**

Give yourself the time you need to grieve the loss of the relationship. I found that my time to grieve was longer than I planned, but it helped me to allow myself time to understand my feelings.

**Step Three**

Watch for triggers that will set you back, i.e., songs that remind you of your relationship. Change the music and do not get in the trap of thinking of just the good times. Keep a list of the things that made you unhappy in your relationship. Keep this list in your phone so you can access the list quickly. If you catch yourself daydreaming about what could have been, use the list as a way to see reality. Keep a list of things people say about you when they describe you or other nice compliments. This list is helpful when you are feeling down. Look at it to keep your attitude up!

**Step Four**

Learn from the relationship. There were some things you did wrong and there were some things that your ex did wrong, but journal about what you will not do in the future. Plan your future by creating a list of what you want and do not want in a future relationship. Learn about the types of love found in the Bible. It is possible that the type of love you felt was not the type that you needed at that particular point in your life. Decide what type of love you want in the future.

**Step Five**

When you run into mutual friends or your ex's family, be kind and show interest in the people you are talking to, but do not ask about your ex or offer reasons for the breakup. If you are told that your ex should have chosen you, just thank them for the compliment. Do not engage in conversations that will set you back.

**Step Six**

Expect that there will be awkward situations and plan ways to handle them. For example, have a plan for when you see friends who do not know about the breakup, see your ex with a date, see pictures of your ex with someone new or when you have to deal with difficult people who are relentless in talking about your ex. The best ways to handle these situations are to be polite but give short statements like, "It did not work out, but I wish my ex well." Ask the people you speak with about their lives and get them talking about themselves or share details about your future and your plans. If they will not move off the breakup topic, excuse yourself and move on.

**Step Seven**

Watch what you let yourself wish for and focus on. Be sure it is about *your* future, not a possible future with your ex. Watch out for "what if" situations. Do not get caught up in "What if I did this" or "What if I just tried one more time." If you really want to move on, try a new activity or a new group to keep yourself busy. In my breakup, I joined a gym and a community organization to help me achieve my new goals of becoming healthier and a better networker.

**Step Eight**

Become your own advocate; guard your heart until you are ready for a relationship. Accept invitations as friends until you are ready to date. Keep busy and remind everyone who wants to set you up that you will attend only as friends. Take the time to get to know yourself before you jump into a relationship. Please learn from me. After a breakup, I missed the attention and love so much that I jumped into a relationship where I thought jealousy was a form of love. I missed the signs that emotional abuse could become physical abuse. If you are lonely, call a friend and surround yourself with positive people who can help. Seek counseling if you are struggling. Do not be afraid to ask for help.

**Step Nine**

Forgive. This will take time, but no matter what the reason for the breakup, you will only be able to truly move on when you can give forgiveness.

**Step Ten**

Search for your faith and lean on God, not on yourself.

**Step Eleven**

Everyone says you can be friends with an ex, but this is your decision and you may need time to move on before you can be friends.

**Step Twelve**

Realize that one day you will wake up and find that you have not thought about your ex. You will someday understand why the relationship did not work out. You will see that what you learned, no matter how difficult, will help you in a future relationship.

# WHAT YOU WANT AND DO NOT WANT IN A RELATIONSHIP

Decide what you want in a relationship. For me, the following list applies.

- Someone who is compassionate and has integrity

- Someone who is fun

- Someone who loves me and makes me a priority

- Someone who helps me achieve my goals

- Someone who believes in me

- Someone who shares my beliefs and values

In regards to what I do not want in a relationship, the following applies.

- Someone who is jealous

- Someone who is selfish

- Someone who is quick to anger

- Someone who holds me back

- Someone who sees me as an option not a priority

- Someone who lets me down and is dishonest

Having a clear sense of what you want and do not want in a relationship is invaluable. Make it a priority to define for yourself what is important to you in a relationship.

# MY JOURNEY JOURNAL

Once you begin a journal, realize that you have choices that can determine how you handle your current situation. As the author of this journal outline, I beg you to choose the right path as you choose how to deal with your situation. I chose the wrong road and a journal helped me determine my feelings and respond to my crisis.

Try to answer the questions with how you honestly feel and then do not react, instead think it over. Read it later and then decide how you will respond.

# YOUR JOURNAL ENTRIES

Describe the crisis or current situation. What happened?

Note today's date and how you feel about the situation.

What do you have to face quickly? What event or place do you have to be at based on this situation?

What will people say to you that may make you angry or sad?

How will you respond when people say the wrong thing?

What do you want people to say and do to help you?

What are you angry about right now?

Do you think you should make some decisions now or wait for awhile?

Are your moods and reactions affecting others?

What is helping you through this situation?

Who are you dependent on?

Do you have guilt about the situation?

How are you dealing with your guilt, anger or grief?

Who do you feel can help you now?

What do you need to take off your schedule right now to help you overcome this situation?

Do you feel you will ever be happy again?

When you have dealt with crisis in the past what helped you?

Are you rushing into anything now?

Do you feel you are making progress today?

Describe what it would look like to handle this situation poorly.

What can happen if you handle things the wrong way?

Do you need help to decide how to handle this situation?

Are there people you know of who have been through what you are going through?

Would it help you to talk to them?

As time has passed how are your feelings changing?

Are your friends and family handling the situation in a healthy way or a destructive way?

How do you feel about how people are handling the crisis?

Do you feel you should be alone or with others when you feel sad or angry?

If you set goals on how you want to handle this crisis, what would they say?

What can you do to help the families and friends closest to the crisis?

What do you want to know and what do you want to not know about the crisis?

How will you use your faith to overcome this situation?

If you lost friends or family in this crisis, write them a note about how you feel and things you want them to know that you did not get to say.

Write a note to family and friends stating how you feel and what you want them to know. You may send or not send the note depending on your situation.

Write a note to the people who caused this crisis and tell them how you feel and ask the questions you want answered.

As time has passed, go back and review this journal. How have your feelings changed?

Did you achieve the goals you wrote down?

Do you need help to achieve your goals?

What would you say to someone who is going through what you went through?

What has helped you?

Do you feel you could help someone in the same situation as you?

Do you feel time has helped you overcome the crisis?

How do you want to remember anyone you may have lost?

If memories are all you have left, write them here so you never forget them.

**Post Traumatic Stress Disorder** *Please visit National Institute of Mental Health for details on what PTSD is and how to get help.*

# THE SECRET WEAPON TO ACHIEVE BALANCE

My friend David Akers taught me how to prioritize my time to achieve more balance through the usage of a calendar program like Microsoft Outlook. With his permission, I can show you how to monitor your choices of how you spend your time. Using the category tabs in MS Outlook, you are able to set up your calendar and add appointments by various colors. You can then see by the amounts of any color exactly how you are balancing your time.

The example below shows my balance of time and goals in an average week. I have seventeen hours in a day so this is how I use the 119 hours I have in a week. The Innovation/Me category of time is usually when I am driving or time when I can think about future projects while listening to music. The Civic category is for networking and meeting new people or helping people I mentor.

- 17 x 7 = 119 total

- Family = 41

- Business = 40

- Teaching = 6

- MBA = 12

- Speaking = 3

- Innovation/Me = 5

- Faith = 4

- Civic = 3

- Fitness = 5

**Successful Study Tips**

**Step One**

Think like the instructor; do what they do. Create questions using the chapters and lecture notes, but do not put in the answers.

**Step Two**

Complete the answers for the questions you created by using keywords that the instructor used in lectures and the author used in textbooks. Instructors grade by looking for keywords that show you know the material.

**Step Three**

Visualize and perform. As you study, see the question and answer in your mind and create a scenario that fits the question and answer. For example, if there are ten steps in a particular sales approach, create a real life example using those steps. Read your question and answer out loud. Actors do this to memorize lines and if you hear something, you can usually remember it and repeat it.

## Step Four

Why miss the points? When you prepare, do not visualize yourself failing. Do not psych yourself out by thinking negative thoughts! Read the question and follow instructions. If asked to describe and define, do both; most students only do one part and miss points. Do not memorize it! Know it! You will need the information in your career, so do not just learn by rote or use the first letter of each section and memorize the letter expecting to know the material! Instead, put the questions in an example so you can see how the information works not by theory, but by practice.

# DEDICATION

This book is dedicated to the only One I follow. The dreams, visions, thoughts and situations have made it clear that You want me to complete this work. My trust is that if only one person finds You then this book brings value. Lord, thank you for opening the doors and leading me to what You want me to do.

To Craig Miracle, only God could have given me my very best friend, husband and an amazing father to our children. Your faith, hard work and patience are an inspiration. "When my soul was in the lost and found, you came along to claim it." Thank you for helping me find my faith. Thank you for mentoring me in my business and showing me how to respect and value my talents. You have believed in me and supported me. You are the dream that I asked God for and I thank you for challenging me to help others through this book. Thank you for understanding me, standing by me, loving me and believing in me.

To MaryAnn Hackenberg, your faith and wisdom inspire me and I love you so very much. I am sorry it took me so long to come to you. You gave me the greatest gift in Dawn.

To Kayla, you are my gift from God and your love gives me my greatest joy.

To Joshua, I believe in you always and love the man you have become.

To my mother, for your strength and grace, thank you for all you have taught me and to my father, who taught me dedication and hard work. Mom and Dad, I am sorry I did not tell you all that happened to me. I wanted to protect you from my hurt. You raised me to be strong and I did not want to let you down.

To Loreen and Lynn, thanks for protecting me, guiding me and listening to me.

To Loreen, Mike, Tom and Lynn, I love you and need you always!

To Kayla, Joshua, Ken, Sandra, Beth, Erica, Karen, Taylor, Alex and Andrew, you are my miracles!

To the Robinson, Donofrio and DeTota families, I love you always!

To Sandra Haskell, my best friend and gift from god. We always said we would be there for each other when love left us. You stayed with me, listened to me and you modeled to me what it means to move forward and respect myself. Your grace, strength and wisdom inspire me every day.

To The Hackenberg, Offredo and McCreery Families, your strength and faith are amazing. My prayer is that you see the impact Dawn and Wendy had and know that I will never ever forget what they taught me.

To Santino Piccoli, San, thank you for understanding and knowing my regret. You are a great man and you help so many people. Your intelligence, fun personality and passion make you incredible and I am blessed for the moments that last a lifetime. I believe in you, BIG TIME. I want all the best for you. You are exceptional!

To Rosie Piccoli, you are awesome, what can I say? You have always been there and you are so special. You mean so much to me and I am blessed with our friendship.

To Missy Wilkinson, I love you, my sister, your words and actions show your spirit and wisdom. Thanks for inspiring me and helping me when I was down. You saw everything through and brought your strength and character. You are all that is loyal and good and I am blessed to be your sister.

To John Kornuta, thank you for saving me and being my hero in the worst time of my life. Thank you for believing in me now and then. Thank you for teaching me forgiveness. Thank you for helping me to become strong enough to publish this book. I am blessed with our friendship. Thank you for making me laugh and showing me joy and adventure.

To Tammy Brown, thanks for being the amazing teacher I hope to be. You are so fun and so smart. You were there for all of this and you journeyed alone to be there for Dawn and Wendy. We all love you, you are the very best of what friendship is and you mean the world to me.

To my mentors, Gerry Chattman, Bruce Akers, Bill Denihan, Phil Stella, Jeanne Hauer, Polly Storm, Hal Becker, Joseph Gustin, Dr. Dudley Turner, Dr. Thomas Vukovich, Ivy Bates, Marcy Hood, Ned Parks, Don Philabaum, Shannon Reilly-Gibb, Virginia Marti Veith,

Lynn Green, Sharon Reed, Len Molloy, Geof Pelia, Andy Hutcherson, Terry Moir and Dr. Vernisha Browne-Boone; your wisdom and strength have helped me grow and become accountable.

To Chris, Laura and Renee, your support and friendship gave me strength to overcome my past. You are always in my heart no matter how far apart we are. I love you so much.

To Bob Pacanovsky, thank you for being a role model for building your life and your business with integrity. Your faith, compassion and grace are an inspiration. Thank you for your support and belief in me and this book. Only your attention to detail could have caught a very important piece I was missing and your help made this a complete work. You helped me then and you help me now, I am blessed with your talent. In the past, you saved me and you did not know how much you influenced me. You showed me how to handle the tough times with faith. I am sure God sent you to me to save me and show me faith and integrity.

To Virginia Marti Veith, you made my dream of teaching come true! Thank you for trusting me and believing in me. Your wisdom, honesty and strength have helped me grow as an instructor. I am honored to have you as a mentor and you have taught me to "Inspect what I expect!" Your faith is an inspiration.

To my VMCAD students, past and present, you are talented, creative and you will change the world. I know I expect a lot from you and you know I am always here to help and provide resources. Thank you for telling me what college students need and that opening my resources to you has helped. You inspired me to help others. I believe in you and I know you will succeed in all you pursue.

To faculty, staff and academic advising at The University of Akron, thank you for helping me and believing in me. I am so sorry I did not listen to your warnings. You picked me up and did not let me fall. Your hard work and talent helped me grow and survive the year the devil loved.

To Advantage Media, Ellie Maas Davis, Alison Morse, Emily Avent and Kim Hall, thank you for inspiring me and challenging me. Your words, support and help have guided me in taking this work from a note about an act of evil to a work that can help people. Thank you for your talent, wisdom and guidance.

Class of 2009

Katherine Miracle M.B.A  University of Phoenix

Kayla Miracle Wadsworth High School

Katherine Miracle

KatherineMiracle.com

MiracleResources.com

km@miracleresources.com

(330) 777-2003 (ext 100)

Share this incredible book with a friend.

Discovering Your Dawn is available through:

**www.katherinemiracle.com**

**http://www.miracleresources.com**

TreeNeutral

Printed in the USA
CPSIA information can be obtained
at www.ICGtesting.com
JSHW012041140824
68134JS00033B/3184